The Author / Kenneth Boa is well equipped by training and experience to write this book. He holds a Bachelor of Science degree (1967) from Case Institute of Technology, Cleveland, Ohio, and graduated with honors from Dallas Theological Seminary (Th.M., 1972). At Dallas he received the C. F. Lincoln Award in Bible Exposition, the Rollin Thomas Chafer Award in Apologetics, and the W. E. Hawkins, Jr. Award in Christian Service.

Presently Ken Boa is director of research and publications for New Life, Inc., an organization that reaches adults for Christ through friendship evangelism. In this work he often talks with college students and older adults who are perplexed by the doctrines considered in this book. "It will be a valuable aid to me," says Boa, "since now I will be able to tell a person puzzled about the Trinity, for example, 'Read chapter 3, and then let's talk about it.'"

Married to the former Karen Rose Powelson, Boa lives in Knoxville, Tenn. He and his wife are parents of one daughter, Heather Robin, born in 1972.

Acknowledgement

I would like to express my gratitude to New Life, Inc. for the freedom to write this book in addition to my other New Life ministries.

GOD,
I DON'T UNDERSTAND

Kenneth Boa

While this book is designed for the reader's personal enjoyment and profit, it is also intended for group study. A leader's guide with visual aids (Victor Multi-use Transparency Masters) is available from your local bookstore or from the publishers at $1.95.

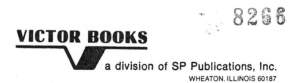

VICTOR BOOKS

a division of SP Publications, Inc.
WHEATON. ILLINOIS 60187

Unless otherwise noted, Scripture quotations are from the *New American Standard Bible* (NASB), © 1971, The Lockman Foundation, LaHabra, Calif., used by permission. Other versions used are the King James Version (KJV); *The Living Bible* (LB), © by Tyndale House Publishers, Wheaton, Ill., used by permission; and *The New International Version: New Testament* (NIV), © 1973, The New York Bible Society International, used by permission.

Cover photo: The Orion Nebula, or M42, is composed mainly of hydrogen gases. According to some astronomers, its critical density is about that which is required for star formation, and scientists are watching M42 for clues to actual suns that may be forming. M42 can be seen without optical aid as a reddish "star" in the constellation Orion. Photograph by the Kitt Peak National Observatory. Used by permission.

Fourth printing, 1977

Library of Congress Catalog Card Number: 75-173
ISBN: 0-88207-722-8

© 1975 by SP Publications, Inc. World rights reserved
Printed in the United States of America

VICTOR BOOKS
A division of SP Publications, Inc.
P. O. Box 1825 ● Wheaton, Ill. 60187

Contents

TO KAREN

"Her worth is far above jewels"
(Proverbs 31:10)

Foreword

Here is good theology in understandable language. Not all writers can accomplish this. Either the theology is so diluted as to make it not worth the time to read, or the language in which it is expressed is so complicated as to make it unintelligible to ordinary mortals like most of us.

Ken Boa has written clearly on some very important subjects which we ought to be thinking about. The author was one of those not-too-common students who stimulated me as a teacher. I recall with pleasure many provocative conversations with him in and out of the classroom. His range of knowledge, thoughtful approach to problems, and clear explanations which I enjoyed during those times together are clearly displayed in this book.

Each chapter makes its own particular contribution to stretching your mind. I wanted to add "but don't miss the ones on sovereignty versus responsibility or space or the Bible"; but if I say that, I hope no one will think the other chapters are somehow less important, for that is not so.

It is a pleasure to commend this book for reading and study. The investment of time will pay good dividends.

CHARLES C. RYRIE
Professor of Systematic Theology
Dallas Theological Seminary
Dallas, Texas

1 What's the Problem?

Most people seem to pass through this short life without ever stopping to consider how profound and mysterious the universe really is. We throw around terms like *energy, time, space, gravity,* and *matter* as though we know what they mean. We get into our routines of life and take things for granted, asking few questions. But underlying all this, a tremendous uncertainty and often a deep desire to find some solid ground exists.

On the other hand, millions have discovered the joy of satisfied desire—they have found and handled the solid ground. It comes in the form of a priceless gift which is free to all who will receive it.

If a powerful being suddenly appeared and offered you a strange box claiming that it contained the answers to many of the secrets of the universe, would you be interested? Assuming you could overcome your impulse to run and that you knew the creature was not diabolical, you would probably be quite anxious to take a look into the box. After all, who would not like to learn the mysteries of the cosmos and discover the blueprints for life if they were so readily available?

The living God has done even more for us than this hypothetical being with the box. He has given us a written revelation that we can keep in our custody, examine, study, and share. God loves us so much that He chose to let us in on some eternal secrets of the universe. The Bible, God's revelation, lets us know *why men exist and how they should live.*

Today men still seek answers to the questions raised since antiquity: Who am I? Where did I come from and where am I going? Are there any absolutes? Apart from God's revelation— His Word—the quest for these answers is futile.

The pursuit of philosophy has led men to anti-philosophy, cynicism, and despair. Men of great intellectual ability find little ground for agreement because their solutions are only speculations. Their answers to the basic questions are simply descents into a pool of unfounded faith.

People hunger for meaning in life. That hunger is unsatisfied, even aggravated, by vain attempts to find meaning in the occult, mysticism, analysis, philosophy, and introspection. Because of our sinful pride, it is difficult for us to receive anything from God simply as a free gift. When God tells us that the real questions and answers are in the Bible, it offends our pride. It sounds too easy. We would rather discover the hidden knowledge, the answers of the elite. Egotistically, we hope that the profundities of life can be mastered by unaided human reasoning.

Those of us who know the Lord Jesus Christ are persuaded that He has the words of eternal life. By His grace we have finally realized that the answers to men's questions have been revealed and that a relationship with the living God is available to all as a free gift. One of the last things Moses said before his death was, "The secret things belong to the Lord our God, but the things revealed belong to us and to our sons forever" (Deut. 29:29).

The man who believes God's Word does not end up in intellectual suicide. Instead his mind rises to heights that he previously could not have attained. He receives supernatural revelation from an all-knowing Creator. When a man starts with the Bible as a foundation for truth and builds upon this, his reasoning is not stifled but stimulated. We are encouraged by the Author of life to erect our superstructures in all disciplines, including science, psychology, and art, but to do so on the biblical foundation of truth.

Speculation or Authority

It is important for us to start with the proper assumptions or presuppositions about life. No matter how wonderful and consistent a system may seem, if it is built upon false premises the entire edifice is doomed to destruction. The Christian does not build upon the speculations of men but upon the revelation of God. His presupposition about life is profoundly simple: "I believe that God has revealed Himself to men, and that revelation is the Bible." Everything he believes about mankind, evil, the future of the universe, God, and salvation comes out of this one presupposition. The child of God begins with the idea that truth is what God says about a thing, and that what He has said is in the Bible.

When a man starts with this simple presupposition, he is released from the limits and uncertainty of his own poor wisdom. He can joyfully allow God's greater wisdom to direct his steps (see 1 Cor. 1:21, 25). The Christian realizes that he has started with something greater than himself intellectually. Thus he has freedom to examine the world and all that is in it, being confidently assured of who made it, how it got here, and why.

The wonderful thing about God's revelation is that He couches infinite truth in finite language. The Bible, like its Author, can never be boring to the one who studies it carefully, because it will take an eternity to search out its heights and depths.

This infinite depth of truth is made possible because God, not man, initiated the process. The Apostle Peter made this point clear when he wrote, "No prophecy of Scripture is a matter of one's own interpretation, for no prophecy was ever made by an act of human will, but men moved by the Holy Spirit spoke from God" (2 Peter 1:20-21).

God tells us we should expect the revelation from Him, the infinite, omniscient Creator, to contain corresponding infinite depth. " 'For My thoughts are not your thoughts, neither are your ways My ways,' declares the Lord. 'For as the heavens are higher than the earth, so are My ways higher than your ways, and My thoughts than your thoughts' " (Isa. 55:8-9).

It's Beyond Us

It follows from all this that men cannot and should not expect to understand the Bible exhaustively. If they could, the Bible would not be divine but limited to human intelligence. A very important idea comes out of this, something over which many non-Christians and even Christians stumble: *Since the Bible is an infinite revelation, it often brings the reader beyond the limit of his intelligence.*

As simple as the Bible is in its message of sin and of free salvation through Christ, an incredible subtlety and profundity underlies all its doctrines. Even a child can receive Christ as his Saviour, thereby appropriating the free gift of eternal life. Yet no philosopher has more than scratched the surface regarding the things that happened at the cross. The Bible forces any man to crash into the ceiling of his own comprehension, beyond which he cannot go until he sees the Lord face to face.

Until a person recognizes that his own wisdom and intelligence are not enough, he is not ready to listen to God's greater wisdom. Jesus alluded to this when He said to God, "Thou didst hide these things from the wise and intelligent and didst reveal them to babes" (Luke 10:21).

These ideas can be depicted by contrasting the mental ability of a dog with that of a man. The ability of a dog may be thought of as consisting of a limited number of bits of information that it is capable of handling. A man also has a limited number of bits of information, but he is capable of storing and working with a good deal more than his dog.

There is some overlap between the mental faculties of a dog and those of a man. The dog may be able to relate to its master's eating of food. It no doubt has a great deal more difficulty trying to understand what its master is doing when he keeps staring at pieces of paper and slowly turning the pages of a book. Though a dog cannot relate to many of the things its owner does, there is enough common ground for limited communication, and a man can teach his pet. There is also enough common ground for man to love a dog, without having an attitude of condescension.

This area of overlap is very important, especially as regards communication. It is almost impossible for anyone to love or train something like a worm or a leech. Why? Because there is no communication.

When a man does something beyond the comprehension of an animal, it must remain a mystery to that animal since it has no categories it can use to correlate this behavior. A dog can be taught to fetch the morning newspaper regularly, but it is another matter to teach it how to read it.

The corresponding analogy between man and God is valid as well. However, the gap is even greater because we must compare man's finite mental capacity to the Lord's boundless capacity.

Even so, God can still communicate real truth to us, and we can communicate with Him, though on a limited level. As Francis Schaeffer has pointed out, He has communicated truly to men though not exhaustively. There are a myriad things that He can comprehend but we cannot grasp. As suggested before, since the Bible is God's revelation to man, it should not be surprising that some of these areas have been implied or directly stated in His revelation.

What's an Antinomy? (an-tin'ə-mi)

We need to come up with a name for such revealed incomprehensibles in order to more easily refer to this concept. The word *paradox* is not the best choice since it often implies only an *apparent* contradiction. *Paradox* is often used for a semantic or a verbal contradiction. In this case we can change the words in such a way as to eliminate the contradiction.

One example from the Scriptures of such a paradox is Paul's statement, "When I am weak, then I am strong" (2 Cor. 12:10). The paradox can be resolved by rewording it: "The less I have, the more I depend on Him" (LB).

The word *oxymoron* is also inappropriate since it is simply a combination of contradictory or incongruous words (*heavy lightness* or *cruel kindness*). This is more a literary device than a description of two contradictory concepts which can both be true at once.

We need a word which describes the fact that God's revelation to man sometimes goes beyond the level of human reasoning and comprehension by stating as factual two things which men cannot reconcile. The word *antinomy* describes these phenomena in God's Word. *Antinomy* is defined by Webster as "a contradiction between two equally valid principles or between inferences correctly drawn from such principles."

This word can be broken down into two parts: *anti* (against) and *nomos* (law), and it simply means "against the law" of human reasoning. What is quite comprehensible to God may be "antinomial" to man. Some things in the Scriptures may be difficult to comprehend, others may be obvious antinomies, and still others may only be possible antinomies.

While the word *antinomy* is not found in the Scriptures or in use as a theological term, it may still be a useful and accurate term to describe some things in the Bible which are beyond or against human reason. Two of the more obvious antinomies which will be considered in this book are the Trinity and the divine/human nature of Jesus Christ.

Antinomies are relative, not absolute. What is antinomial to a dog may be quite comprehensible to a man, and what is antinomial with respect to human reasoning may be comprehensible to beings with greater powers of reasoning (angels and God).

Because Christ conquered sin and death, the degeneration of man and of the universe due to man's fall will be reversed when He comes again. Our ability to comprehend God's truth will then be increased, and it is likely that we will understand many of the things that are now antinomies. "For now we see in a mirror dimly, but then face to face; now I know in part, but then I shall know fully just as I also have been fully known" (1 Cor. 13:12).

Beware of Explanations

An important thing to remember is that, because of its very nature, *we cannot illustrate or explain an antinomy.* When we are working with a real antinomy, even good illustrations will fall short of a complete clarification. Accepting such explanations as complete can lead to error and a lack of balance. While illustrations may be helpful in clarifying the two ideas which appear on a human level to be contradictory, they should not be given with the impression that they will provide an adequate solution to the riddle itself.

The Christian, therefore, must realize his need for faith in God's revealed Word. His human wisdom must be placed in a position subordinate to God's revelation. It would be the height of egotism for a person to say that because an idea in the Bible does not make sense (does not conform to his reasoning), it cannot be true and the Bible must be in error on this point. Yet, men try to judge the Bible instead of letting it judge them. They try to approach God on their own terms, wanting to tell Him how to operate and who to be.

When a person insists on trying to subject the two contradictory elements contained in a biblical antinomy to human comprehension, he will inevitably, though perhaps subtly, move to one extreme or to the other. The only way to rationalize an antinomy is to remove the tension between the two contradictory elements by essentially ignoring one or the other. Either we will enlarge idea A out of proportion and minimize idea B, or vice versa.

We need to understand both elements in each antinomy, while resisting our natural temptation to remove the tension produced. To maintain a proper balance we should accept the tension by supporting both ideas involved equally. This is, of course, unnatural, and it is here that faith in God's revealed Word must govern us.

It is not a "cop-out" to accept both ideas of a biblical antinomy by faith without continually looking for some rationalization or explanation. It would only be a cop-out if we were dealing with a difficult theological concept rather than an antinomy. It is important therefore to distinguish between the two to determine how to approach a given problem.

Antinomies require precise statement and analysis. The improper choice of a word or phrase could introduce an error by overemphasizing one of the two ideas involved in the antinomy. This is true of all theology since the words used, even so-called "insignificant" words, will sometimes affect large meanings. This is not a matter of wrangling over words, but simply the nature of theology.

This preciseness of language can be found throughout the Scriptures since God inspired not only the ideas but also the words involved. For example, Paul builds a whole argument upon the ending of one word from an Old Testament reference (see Gal. 3:16).

Truth is Complex

Another interesting thing about antinomies is that they seem to touch upon every major area of theology. In fact, an examination of antinomies is simply a different way of looking at theology.

This does not mean that the basic doctrines of Scripture are not clear, for they certainly are. The biblical account of the origin of sin, the nature of God as an omniscient, sovereign, eternal Being, the details of the creative and the redemptive work of the Lord, and the ultimate future of man are all clearly spelled out.

However, these very doctrines and others, when more closely examined, show forth a tremendous subtlety and complexity which can ultimately defy analysis. Back of all these doctrines is a simple and yet immensely complex reality.

This same complexity may be observed also in nature because everything that exists derives its being from God Himself. The Scriptures say of the Lord Jesus, "All things have been created through Him and for Him. And He is before all things, and in Him all things hold together" (Col. 1:16-17).

An in-depth study of any part of God's creation illustrates this complexity. Things which may appear to be clear and simple display astonishing depths of intricacy and involvement. The more closely a flower or a leaf is examined, the more marvelous it becomes. Thus, a study of the antinomial things of God's written revelation can be both profitable and humbling. It can lead to a greater awe and appreciation of the One who has allowed all who believe in Him to be members of His own household.

Heresy Results from Oversimplification

Another reason to study antinomies is to avoid the misunderstandings that result in false teaching. Wrong theology and many heretical cults have arisen over the centuries out of a lack of balance with respect to antinomies. False teaching results when men stumble over important antinomies (such as the Trinity and the God-man) without recognizing them as such.

When a person discovers an antinomy, he may try to avoid it instead of acknowledging it for what it is. He refuses to believe that both concepts contained within the antinomy are true at once. This is based on the idea that if something doesn't make sense to natural logic, it certainly cannot be true. This idea becomes the foundation stone for erroneous systems of doctrine. The error generally consists in overemphasizing one idea at the expense of its counterpart.

Another common solution people use to avoid antinomies is the convenient adjustment of their method of interpreting the Bible. That is, if the ideas contained in scriptural passages do not make sense based on a normal literal interpretation, some people spiritualize or allegorize the passages involved. They simply refuse to acknowledge the obvious meaning of the text because it does not fit in with their preconceived notions. Antinomies are therefore closely related to Bible interpretation because carelessness in one area will produce carelessness in the other.

The Jehovah's Witnesses are an example of how trying to rationalize or avoid antinomies in the Bible produces false teaching and cultism. They reject the doctrine of the Trinity because it does not make sense to them that God could be three persons and yet one God in essence. This admittedly runs against the grain of human reasoning (that is why it is called an antinomy), and a natural human tendency would be to avoid the problem by holding a unitarian view of God.

The simple reasoning involved is that since God is one He cannot consist of three persons. The next step then is to impose this viewpoint upon all the Scripture, twisting it to avoid the fact of the deity and/or personality of Jesus Christ and the Holy Spirit. In this case as in many others, the refusal to accept what is by nature an antinomy has led directly to serious errors in interpretation and theology.

A sensitivity to the implications of biblical antinomies can be both corrective and preventive medicine. It can correct false teaching by providing a more open and less biased approach to the Scriptures. It can also prevent the encroachment of error by giving people an understanding of why and how error slips in unnoticed.

A Mark of Divinity

The fact that the Bible contains antinomies is good evidence of its divine origin. If it were not inspired of God, the teachings contained in it would be limited to human intelligence, imagination, and reason.

The question then arises, what about scriptures from other religions? Books like the *Koran* and the *Bhagavad Gita,* as well as cultic books like the *Book of Mormon* and *Science and Health* contain few real antinomies, and in some cases none. Many of these books in fact rehash the Bible to remove the biblical antinomies because of the difficulties they produce. Other scriptures like to get rid of things like the Trinity, the God-man, and the problem of divine sovereignty versus human responsibility. They may include paradoxical notions in order to build a fabric of the mysterious and the enigmatic, but these notions do not ultimately defy human reasoning.

The wonderful and unique thing about the Bible is that it is full of things men would never have dreamed up. Many of its messages are the last things people would want to write. The fact is that antinomies by their very nature produce insoluble problems, just the sort of problems that would keep people from considering the Bible at all apart from a supernatural intervention.

However, we must be very careful here, because this is not to say that the things revealed in God's Word are illogical. All the ideas which can be comprehended in the Bible make wonderful sense. But there are other concepts which, while not contrary to human reason, do go beyond it. That is to say, the Bible frequently shows evidence of a logic and an understanding which is superior to anything presently attainable by mankind.

A Tool for Apologetics

Another practical reason for the study of antinomies is their apologetic value, because their presence in the Bible is the ultimate basis for many non-Christian objections to Christianity. A study of this type can help us more clearly understand why non-Christians may have trouble with the message of the Gospel. We begin to see how absolutely important it is for us to rely on the convicting ministry of the Holy Spirit when witnessing to those who do not know the Saviour.

Some antinomies have a more practical value in terms of the everyday Christian life and witnessing than others. Two which affect us directly are those dealing with the problem of evil and the nature of salvation.

Other antinomies seem to be more abstract, not relating closely to everyday life. Because of this they do not cause as many problems and are easily acceptable. Most people have fewer difficulties with the nature of time and the resurrection body than they do with divine sovereignty versus human freedom and responsibility. But since these concepts are equally antinomial, Christians should remember that the ones they find harder to accept are in reality no more difficult than the ones that do not bother them.

Seven Reasons for Studying Antinomies

To summarize, there are at least seven practical values of a study of antinomies in the Bible:

1. It shows that reason must be subject to God's revelation. A strong faith in all of Scripture is essential, for only in this way can intellectual satisfaction regarding the difficult portions of God's Word be achieved.

2. It helps Christians maintain a balance in critical areas of

biblical theology, and, in fact, provides a different perspective to the study of theology.

3. It gives a greater appreciation for God and His Word because it shows something of the profound depth and ineffable mysteries involved. This is very humbling for the child of God and should result in praise and worship of our eternal Father.

4. It provides insight into the production of false teaching throughout the centuries and shows how it can and should have been avoided. It also illustrates the need for a proper and consistent interpretation of the Bible.

5. It displays the uniqueness and divine origin of the Scriptures.

6. It can become a valuable aid in witnessing to non-Christians because the presence of antinomies and the problems they cause to the natural mind are part of the basis for unbelieving objections to Christianity.

7. It can have a practical value for the daily Christian walk. It can affect a Christian's outlook on life and therefore his behavior.

One danger to avoid is discovering antinomies where they don't really exist. One can search so hard for antinomies that he exaggerates things which are only difficulties to an antinomial level. Some subjects included in this study as antinomies may be debatable and are so labelled. The primary example of this is the one related to space (the creation). This is a possible antinomy, but not dogmatically so classified. It has been included because a consideration of it may be helpful and consistent with our purpose.

It is important to realize that just because something is called an antinomy. does not mean that we may nonchalantly set it aside without any further thought or discussion. This could lead to the pious "just take it by faith" attitude, when in reality these things demand continued thought and periodic reevaluation.

Just as one or more of the subjects discussed in this study may not absolutely be antinomial, there may be (and probably are) one or more genuine biblical antinomies which have not been included.

An appreciation of these wonders of God's revelation can lead to a greater comprehension of the uniqueness, wisdom, and depth of the Bible and, correspondingly, of the One who inspired it. This subject relates directly to the two great works that God has done for which He deserves and is to receive all praise, honor, worship, and dominion forevermore: His loving work of creation and His redemption of that creation.

2　The God-Man

Jesus Christ Himself, the central figure of Christianity, represents a biblical antinomy. Many portions of Scripture completely affirm His deity, showing that at no time did He lose His divine nature. Yet the Bible teaches, equally strongly, that Christ became fully human.

His Deity

Christ receives divine titles in the Word of God. The familiar prologue to the Gospel of John reads, "In the beginning was the Word, and the Word was with God, and *the Word was God*." John makes it clear that this Word is Jesus Christ: "And the Word became flesh, and dwelt among us, and we beheld His glory, glory as of the only begotten from the Father, full of grace and truth" (John 1:14). Jesus Christ is therefore called God in John 1:1.

The same is true of this passage: "But of the Son He says, 'Thy throne, *O God,* is forever and ever, and the righteous scepter is the scepter of His kingdom' " (Heb. 1:8).

Paul addresses Christ as God when he says, "Looking for the blessed hope and the appearing of the glory of our great God and Saviour, Christ Jesus" (Titus 2:13; see 2 Peter 1:1).

The Gospel of John records Thomas' response to the resurrected Christ: "Thomas answered and said to Him, 'My Lord and my God!' " (John 20:28)

Jesus Christ is called the Son of God in numerous passages

(Luke 3:22; Matt. 16:15-17; John 10:36). He is also called Lord in many passages (1 Cor. 12:3; Phil. 2:11).

Jesus Christ not only accepted worship due only to God but also demanded it (Matt. 4:10; John 5:23). Christ claimed to be the supreme object of faith, demanding of men the same kind of faith which they placed in God (John 17:1-3). He said, "I and the Father are one" (John 10:30).

The scriptural case for the fact that Jesus Christ is God is further supported by Christ's divine attributes and works. He is eternal (John 17:5; Heb. 1:11-12), omnipresent (Matt. 28:20), and omnipotent (Heb. 1:3). The Scriptures show Him to be the Creator of all things (John 1:3; Col. 1:16; Heb. 1:2), and the One who holds all things in the universe together (Col. 1:17; Heb. 1:3). He alone as God offers forgiveness of sins (Luke 5:20-24), and all men will face Him in judgment (John 5:24-28). Thus, the fact of Christ's full deity has clear biblical support.

His Humanity
The Bible builds an equally clear case in support of Christ's full humanity subsequent to the incarnation. Several passages indicate that Christ had a human birth (Matt. 1:18-25; Luke 2:4-21; John 1:14; 1 Tim. 3:15; 1 John 4:1-3). He also had a human development (Luke 2:52). He had all the human elements: a body (John 2:21), a soul (John 12:27), and a spirit (Luke 23:46).

In addition, just as Christ had divine names, He also had human names such as "man" (1 Tim. 2:5), "Son of man" (Luke 19:10), and "Son of David" (Mark 10:47). Christ possessed all of the human limitations except sin. He got tired, hungry, thirsty, sorrowful, and He died.

The Bible therefore gives clear testimony to the humanity as well as the complete deity of Jesus Christ. Paul summarizes this: "For in Him all the fulness of Deity dwells in bodily form" (Col. 2:9).

The antinomy here lies in the fact that humanity is not the same as deity. If Jesus were 50% God and 50% man (as some have taught) there would be no problem, since one-half plus one-half equals one. But the Bible does not allow this because it testifies that Jesus is a total man and fully God. Even though it is easy to make a statement like this, there is no way in which it can be truly comprehended since one plus one does not equal one. It is like trying to put one quart of water and one quart of oil into a one-quart container.

Human reasoning denies that one can be fully human and fully divine, but the Bible tells us that is the case with Jesus Christ.

Three Alternatives

When someone realizes that the Scriptures reveal Christ to be the complete God-man, he has three basic alternatives. First, he may decide to reject this revelation because it does not make sense to him. Such a rejection would diminish or completely erase the authority of the Word of God in his mind.

Second, he can try to reason it out, reword it, or illustrate it, as though it could be resolved like a paradox. In this case the issue is skirted by minimizing certain Scriptures or avoiding a direct collision with the implications of the biblical data on this point.

The third alternative is to acknowledge that no analogies or illustrations will really solve the puzzle, and that the complete authority of the Word of God must be recognized, no matter how difficult some of its implications may be. All the biblical data is accepted by faith, and reason is made subject to revelation. Only when the Bible is approached in this way can intellectual satisfaction be attained.

There is a parallel to this in the area of salvation. A person without Christ will not rid himself of his doubts about Christianity until he decides to receive Christ into his life by faith. Satisfaction and peace then follow as a natural by-product.

It is unfortunate that, historically, most people confronted by this antinomy have chosen one or the other of the first two alternatives. They have either rejected the biblical testimony concerning the God-man or they have juggled or ignored certain passages in an attempt to make this compatible with human comprehension. This has led to two inevitable extremes.

One extreme is to reject the deity of Jesus Christ, thus reducing Him to the level of being a man only. Often people will try to reduce the thrust of this approach by throwing in a few kind words. They say that Jesus was indeed a "great teacher" or a "true prophet." Statements like these shouldn't fool anyone since almost all false systems want to give lip-service to Jesus and put Him on their bandwagon in spite of their rejection of His deity.

The implications of this extreme undermine all of Christianity. It would mean among other things that the Bible is not true and salvation is still not available, since the death of a mere man (no matter how noble he may have been) cannot provide the infinite purchase price required to redeem other men from their sins. This would leave all of us in deep trouble, since no one can hope to please a holy God with his own efforts.

This first extreme viewpoint concerning the God-man would imply that it is an utter waste of time to study the Scriptures and get into Christianity at all. If Christ is not God, the Bible is wrong, there is no salvation, and each man must become his own authority for "truth."

The opposite extreme is equally devastating. In this case the deity of Christ is affirmed, but His humanity is minimized or rejected. Interestingly, the results of this extreme are essentially the same as those of the first extreme. The Bible would not be the Word of God, and salvation would not be available for men.

Since the Bible makes it clear that Jesus Christ was completely human, a rejection of His humanity is tantamount to a rejection of the Bible. And salvation would not be available because the substitutionary atonement requires that Jesus Christ must die as a man to bear judgment for the sins of all men. As Scripture says, "There is one God, and one mediator also between God and men, the man Christ Jesus, who gave Himself as a ransom for all, the testimony borne at the proper time" (1 Tim. 2:5-6). The Messiah could not have become the mediator between God and man apart from becoming the God-man by taking on human flesh. Many other important biblical doctrines would be destroyed with the notion that Christ never became a man, but the two which have been discussed here (God's revelation to man and His provision of a Saviour) are the most critical.

Errors through the Centuries

Church history affords a number of illustrations of how men have tried either to reject or rationalize this God-man antinomy. The two erroneous extremes just discussed have appeared in many forms throughout the centuries and will continue to arise as long as men refuse to bow to the authority of God's revelation of Himself in the Scriptures.

The Gnostics were among the first who perverted the biblical doctrine of the God-man. Because of their dualistic conviction that matter is evil, they refused to believe in the incarnation of Jesus Christ. Theirs was a form of Docetism, a doctrine which taught that Christ only *seemed* to have a real body. They believed that Christ tricked the evil god of the Old Testament at the crucifixion because His body was not real.

The Apostle John fought against the developing Gnosticism of his day and urged his readers to "test the spirits," for "every spirit that confesses that Jesus Christ has come in the flesh is from God; and every spirit that does not confess Jesus is not from God" (1 John 4:1-3; see 2 John 7). John was vehemently opposed to this denial of the full humanity of Jesus, calling it "the spirit of the antichrist."

Another controversy related to the issue of the God-man was generated in part by Arius of Alexandria in the early 4th century. Arius said that Christ was different from God and was of another substance. The conflict which arose from this led to the important Council of Nicea in A.D. 325.

Opposition to the deity of Christ was soon followed by a return to the other extreme. Apollinaris held a docetic view of Christ, saying that Christ was not truly human. Apollinaris placed his reason above Scripture and refused to accept that both the human and the divine nature were in Christ.

Nestorius was another church leader who stumbled over this antinomy. He ended up with two persons, saying that Jesus as a man was energized by the *logos* of God. This was effectively a denial of the complete deity of Jesus Christ.

Eutyches in the 5th century arrived at the unusual viewpoint that Christ was neither truly human nor divine, but was a *"tertium quid"* (a "third other").

Following this, there arose the Monophysite group which stressed the divine nature in Christ and minimized His human nature to such an extent that His humanity was divested of all but a few human characteristics. That represented another swing back to the docetic (not completely human) view of Christ.

Though representatives of both extremes regarding the God-man continued to persist, the major Christological controversies beginning with the 7th century centered more on the work than on the person of Jesus Christ. The next major group to deny the deity of Christ in favor of His humanity were the Socinians in the 16th century. Since that time the most common trend in avoiding the God-man antinomy has been a simple rejection of the biblical testimony concerning the deity of Christ. This has been supported in large measure by 18th- and 19th-century philosophy, the evolutionary hypothesis, and higher criticism. The docetic extreme of minimizing the true humanity of Christ was more common in the days of the Early Church and is not often found today.

Other False Views of Christ

Outside of the main lines of church history, many more examples of the two extremes (a denial of Christ's deity or of His humanity) can be found by looking into the beliefs of cults and eastern religions concerning the person of Jesus Christ. Several of these religions regard Christ as simply another prophet sent by God to help enlighten the people of His day. Along with this goes the claim that other prophets with an even greater message have succeeded Jesus, and people of today should first listen to them (for instance, Muhammad, Baha'u'llah, and more recently, Sun Myung Moon). Other groups think of Jesus as "divine" in the same pantheistic sense in which all men are divine, thus rejecting Christ's exclusive claims.

Another popular approach which has been supported by various esoteric and occult teachings is the separation of Jesus from Christ. This is an old idea which goes back to 2nd- and 3rd-century Monarchianism. Men like Paul of Samosata taught that "the Christ" (the divine power) descended upon the man Jesus at His baptism and left Him just prior to His crucifixion. This has been extended by some today into the idea that all of us can have this divine power or "Christ Consciousness" within us.

All these erroneous teachings concerning the God-man place faith in human reason above God's revelation. Thus it is imperative for each true believer in Christ to accept by faith all the scriptural data. He must not rationalize or disregard those elements which tax his comprehension, or he will be guilty of subjectively choosing those parts of the Bible he likes and eliminating the rest.

Some Related Issues

At this point, it may be helpful to deal specifically with some of the practical problems and questions related to the God-man antinomy. Remember, since these problems are related directly to antinomial content, by definition there can be no really satisfying solutions to them on a human level. They only illustrate the nature and implications of the antinomy of the God-man.

One related issue is the preexistence and eternality of Christ prior to His incarnation. Many Old and New Testament passages make it clear that Christ existed before He was born of Mary and that there never was a time when Christ was not (Micah 5:2; John 1:1-2; 8:58).

Christ has always existed without a body apart from time and space as equal with the Father and with the Holy Spirit. He was always the Son of God by eternal generation from the Father.[1]

Yet, while He is the same One who has forever existed, in another way He is different. Before He became man He always possessed a divine nature, but since that time He now possesses a divine-human nature (the word *nature* referring to essential qualities or intrinsic properties). He still subsists as the same Person but He is now a divine-human Person.

This concept that there is now a God-man in heaven and that Christ now has a divine-human nature affects the trinitarian relationship because Christ is part of the Godhead. There is a close relationship between the two antinomies of the God-man and the Trinity. But even though Christ will forever have a body which He never possessed in eternity past, God's immutability remains: He has not changed in His essence or in His subsistence (mode of being).

It was the will or decree of God from the councils of eternity past that Jesus Christ would take on human flesh and human nature in the context of God's space-time creation. This timeless plan provided that Christ would have a divine-human nature while remaining a single personality (see John 1:1-14; 1 John 1:1-3; Phil. 2:6-11). Part of the problem here is the question of what controlled the interaction of these two 100% entities.

It would not be accurate to say that "Jesus did this out of His humanity," or "He did that out of His deity." This would divide the personality of Jesus and imply that the association between Christ's humanity and His deity is mutually exclusive. The real affiliation between the human and the divine in the person of Jesus Christ is an unsolvable mystery, since no one has the intellectual categories which can relate to such a combination.

The concept of God's revelation in Christ, the God-man, was

so overwhelming to the existentialist Kierkegaard [2] that he called it the "Absolute Paradox." This was part of the basis for his "leap of faith" into the unknown, into the fact that cannot be a fact. And even though Kierkegaard acknowledged the God-man antinomy, he used it improperly as a basis for his existential system which all but eliminated the facts of the Bible and history.

The Problem of the Kenosis

The great passage which describes the *kenosis* (self-emptying) of Jesus Christ is Philippians 2:5-11. The *kenosis* is related directly to Christ's nature as God and man, and verses 6-8 portray what was involved. "Although He existed in the form of God, [He] did not regard equality with God a thing to be grasped, but emptied Himself, taking the form of a bondservant, and being made in the likeness of men. And being found in appearance as a man, He humbled Himself by becoming obedient to the point of death, even death on a cross."

Some have tried to argue from this passage that Christ surrendered His deity in becoming a man. These verses do not support this view but instead teach that the union of Christ to unglorified humanity was the supreme picture of His extreme humility and condescension based on His love for men.

Also involved in Christ's self-emptying is His voluntary nonuse of some of His attributes, particularly omniscience, omnipresence, and omnipotence. This does not mean that He surrendered these attributes. He could not do so without losing His deity since these attributes are part of God's nature.

Voluntary nonuse means that He personally willed not to exercise them on most occasions while He was on earth. Christ veiled His resplendent glory from His birth to His ascension, but He was not divested of this intrinsic glory any more than placing a filter over a floodlight diminishes the brightness of the lamp itself. On at least two occasions this veil was taken away for a short time (the Transfiguration and in the Garden of Gethsemane). In summary, the Creator of the heavens and the earth humbled Himself to become a perfect man.

The doctrine of the *kenosis* of Christ raises other questions. One is, How could He have learned anything when He was a child, if He was at the same time the omniscient God? How could it be said that Jesus as God "learned obedience from the things which He suffered"? (Heb. 5:8) The impenetrable answer to this must lie in the nature of how Christ could voluntarily not use His omni-attributes for periods of time. Somehow the omniscient Lord Jesus was able to veil His omniscience from Himself without diminishing His deity or perfection. As a man He required a preparation period before He could begin His public ministry, and it could be said that "Jesus kept increasing in wisdom and stature, and in favor with God and men" (Luke 2:52).

Another question pertinent to Christ's childhood concerns His ability to control His miraculous resources. Jesus needed to mature or "increase" in four basic areas: Intellectually ("wisdom"), physically ("stature"), spiritually and socially ("in favor with God and men"). With respect to His human nature, Christ needed to mature, but from the standpoint of His divine nature Jesus as God cannot mature, but is always perfect.

It is difficult to comprehend how the interaction of Christ's dual nature worked in such a way that He always had perfect physical and mental control over His supernatural abilities.

The idea of a human with superhuman endowment has always intrigued the popular mind. Variations on this theme have been developed in the areas of science fiction (with cyborgs and men of superhuman intelligence), children's comic books and TV shows (especially "super heroes" like Superman), and the alluring promises of supernatural abilities offered by witchcraft, the occult, and the black arts.

In reality, due to the presence of the sin nature, a person's powers are directly proportional to his potential for wickedness and destruction. For example, if a person like Superman really existed, the world or at least a large proportion of mankind would probably have been destroyed long before he reached maturity due to some fit of anger when he was a child. Even if the world did survive his maturation, men everywhere would be gripped by his controlling hand, waiting in dread for his next odious impulse or appetite to become law.

We can thank God that Jesus Christ's limitless abilities were wonderfully controlled and exercised because of His undiminished deity and perfect humanity. Christ was always motivated by love and compassion for men and was incapable of sinning because He could not go against His own nature as God.

Another question which relates to Christ's early childhood and

His voluntary nonuse of His omniscience during most of His time on earth concerns His knowledge of His own person and ministry. How much of His destiny did He know, and when did He realize He was the Messiah? Luke indicates that *at least* by the age of 12 Jesus was clearly aware of His identity as the Son of God (2:49). As for His complete awareness of His mission as the substitutionary sacrifice for the sins of the world, the Gospels show that Jesus had a clear knowledge of this at least by the time He was baptized by John.

Since the Scriptures are mostly silent about Jesus' life before He began his public ministry, a more definite answer to these questions cannot be given. It lies within the mystery of how He could know all things as God and voluntarily choose to limit His knowledge at the same time.

Incidentally, these 18 to 20 "silent years" in Christ's life from age 12 (Luke 2:40-52) to the time of His baptism by John (Luke 3:1-22) have been seized by representatives from various religions, cultic and occult, in an attempt to diminish Christ's deity and reduce Him to the level of a precursor of these false systems.

Some, for instance, have taught that He derived most of His teachings from the Essene community during this period of time. Others say He spent some of these years in India, where He was initiated into the labyrinths of Hinduism. When evidence for this curious viewpoint is requested, they proudly reply that John the Baptist was Jesus' guru!

Several apocryphal books have attempted to spice up these unknown years by ascribing bizarre miracles to Jesus' ministry. This kind of preoccupation with things not revealed in Scripture is misguided, since God has purposely chosen to veil them. The Apostle John said specifically, "And there are also many other things which Jesus did, which if they were written in detail, I suppose that even the world itself would not contain the books which were written" (21:25).

Other enigmatic questions concerning the God-man can be connected with the nature of the virgin birth. One such question might be, At what point before His birth did Jesus become the God-man?

Another passage which has an interesting bearing on the God-man antinomy is the description of Christ's work in Colossians: "For in Him all things were created . . . and in Him all things hold together" (1:16-17). Not only did the Lord Jesus create all things which exist in the universe; He also continues to sustain His entire creation at all times and in all places. If Christ failed to hold creation together for a moment, all things in the heavens and on the earth would undergo atomic dissolution! This is precisely what will happen in the future when God destroys this universe and creates a new and eternal heaven and earth (2 Peter 3:10-13).

There is no way of knowing how the universe is being held together by Christ, but it may be related to the inexplicable force which holds the nuclei of all atoms together. The positively charged particles which are packed so closely together in atomic nuclei might be expected to repel each other because they have the same charge, and yet they remain compact. If this binding force in all atoms were removed, all matter in the universe would come apart, and all things could be reduced to pure energy.

The connection of this passage (Col. 1:16-17) with the God-man antinomy lies in the fact that, since Christ had a human body, He physically was composed of atoms and molecules. Christ therefore must literally have been holding Himself together while on earth! The word translated *hold together (synistemi)* can mean "continue, endure, exist, consist, or be composed" in this context (and in 2 Peter 3:5, where it is also connected with the existence or enduring of the heavens).

After His resurrection, Christ took on a new body of glorified flesh, a body suitable for a heavenly existence (see 1 Cor. 15:42-51). This is the same body that Jesus now possesses in heaven, and though it relates to the antinomy of the resurrection body (see chap. 6), it can still be said that Christ as the self-existent God will forever continue to hold Himself together and maintain His consistence.

One final consideration concerning this antinomy needs to be made. How could Christ be temptable and impeccable (incapable of sinning) at the same time? These two facts are suggested in Hebrews. "For we do not have a high priest who cannot sympathize with our weaknesses, but one who has been tempted in all things as we are, yet without sin" (4:15).

Since being temptable and at the same time being impeccable is antinomial, the only thing we can say is that His temptability is related to His complete humanity and His impeccability is connected with His complete deity. Christ could not have sinned on any occasion for He is God. Yet, Christ was "tempted in all things as we are." The temptation was very real for He was fully human.

How Can Men Model the God-man?

Christians are supposed to model their lives after Christ. "For you have been called for this purpose, since Christ also suffered for you, leaving you an example for you to follow in His steps, who committed no sin, nor was any deceit found in His mouth" (1 Peter 2:21-22; see also 1 Peter 1:14-16).

The question is, How can Christ be our example and model when He was also God? How can we "follow in His steps, who committed no sin"?

To some it seems almost unfair. But Paul says it can be done: "Be imitators of me, just as I also am of Christ" (1 Cor. 11:1). Here he is claiming that his life is so Christlike that others can and should imitate it.

How can a man's life attain this quality? As it is often said, "The Christian life is not difficult—it's impossible!" The solution is seen in Paul's statement, "I have been crucified with Christ; and it is no longer I who live, but Christ lives in me; and the life which I now live in the flesh I live by faith in the Son of God, who loved me, and delivered Himself up for me" (Gal. 2:20). Paul's life of modeling Christ was possible only insofar as he appropriated the power of the indwelling God.

The Christian life, then, is a divine-human process. It is a supernatural, not a natural life. God has not told us "Here are the rules. Good luck!" Instead, all who have received Christ are indwelt by the Father, the Son, and the Holy Spirit (John 14:17-23). Christians are empowered by the eternal Godhead, but we need to allow this power to control and transform our lives by faith.

The God-man's life is, therefore, a valid model for all believers because the living indwelling God offers divine enablement to all Christians who want it. This divine-human process involved in the Christian life is mentioned by Paul, "Work out your salvation with fear and trembling; for it is God who is at work in you, both to will and to work for His good pleasure" (Phil. 2:12-13). Verse 12 describes the human and verse 13 the divine role in the outworking of the Christian life.

The true humanity of Christ is graphically depicted by the author of the Epistle to the Hebrews. "During the days of Jesus' life on earth, He offered up prayers and petitions with loud cries and tears to the One who could save Him from death, and He was heard because of His reverent submission. Although He was a Son, He learned obedience from what He suffered, and once made perfect, He became the source of eternal salvation for all who obey Him" (Heb. 5:7-9, NIV). Christ offered up prayers and "learned obedience," and He was helped and sustained by His heavenly Father. All Christians will do well to follow His example.

A person who is in Christ has the potential to choose not to sin in any given situation. Since he is indwelt by the living God, he can choose to "put on the new self, which in the likeness of God has been created in righteousness and holiness of the truth" (Eph. 4:24).

However, because the old man as well as the new man is still with us, the fact that we can choose not to sin on specific occasions does not mean that we can become sinlessly perfect in this life. The Apostle John makes it clear that until the old nature is removed from believers, we will continue to sin: "If we say that we have no sin, we are deceiving ourselves, and the truth is not in us" (1 John 1:8; see 1:10—2:2). But since we have access to the supernatural power of God by grace through faith, the life of Christ is still a valid example for all of God's children to follow.

3 The Trinity

Theology, the study of God, appears to many to be too presumptuous and ambitious a project. Even some theologians cut off the branch they are sitting on by denying that any genuine study can be made of God. How can we who are finite speak meaningfully about the infinite? How can the inscrutable and incomprehensible be described in human terms?

Philosopher Paul Tillich even went so far as to say that God is beyond existence and beyond supernaturalism. For Tillich, the question of God's existence is out of order, let alone the possibility of knowing specific things about Him.[1] This kind of approach, for him, can only lead to negative results: what God is *not*.

As long as man sets up his own mind as the standard for truth, he cannot attain a real knowledge of God. The problem of knowing God is solved in one word: revelation. When God's Word instead of unaided human reasoning becomes the basis for truth, answers are possible.

The Problem

Because the living God has revealed Himself to us, we can make positive and specific statements about Him based on this revelation. We can confidently describe many of His attributes, such as holiness, justice, love, and immutability. Though we will never know all there is to know about God, we can be satisfied that the things He has told us about Himself in the Bible are true.

Moreover, those who have trusted in Christ know God in a personal as well as an intellectual way.

Nevertheless, Christians recognize that there are many things about God which are mysterious, incomprehensible, and superrational. God in His existence as the Three-in-One is beyond the limits of human comprehension.

The Scriptures reveal not only the complete unity of the Godhead but also the equally complete distinctiveness of the three Persons who make up the Godhead. Through all eternity there is a perfect and absolute unity and diversity because the Godhead is One and Three.

The term *Trinity* is generally used to describe the Godhead. The *tri* emphasizes God's threeness and the *nity* emphasizes His unity. He is a "Triunity." Although the term *Trinity* is not found in Scripture, this does not prohibit its usefulness in the study of God's revealed nature.

Scriptural Proof for the Trinity

We can demonstrate the Trinity of God by giving biblical evidence first for His unity and then for His threeness. We shall then complete this evidence by looking at some verses which combine these two truths.

It is clear from both the Old and New Testaments that there is but one God, not three. "You shall have no other gods before Me" (Ex. 20:3; Deut. 5:7) is the first of the Ten Commandments. One of the clearest and best known statements of God's unity is, "Hear, O Israel! The Lord is our God, the Lord is one!" (Deut. 6:4)

Isaiah writes, "Remember the former things long past, for I am God, and there is no other; I am God, and there is no one like Me" (46:9; see also Deut. 32:39). "Before Me there was no God formed, and there will be none after Me" (Isa. 43:10).

New Testament passages such as 1 Corinthians 8:4-6, Ephesians 4:4-6, and James 2:19 also reveal the fact that "there is no God but one" (1 Cor. 8:4).

Nevertheless, God is also three. Even the Old Testament implies that the unity of God is a corporate unity. God revealed Himself to man in a progressive way during some 1500 years over which the Bible was written. The Old Testament often implies what the New Testament declares explicitly.

Several important hints in the Old Testament foreshadow the New Testament revelation of the three-in-oneness of God. One of these is the name *Elohim* which is translated *God* but is plural in number.

There are also many instances of God using the plural pronoun to describe Himself: "Then God said, 'Let Us make man in Our image, according to Our likeness'" (Gen. 1:26; also compare Gen. 3:22; 11:7; Isa. 6:8).

Another strong hint for the Trinity of God relates to the person of the Messiah. Isaiah reveals Him to be an equal with God, calling Him the "Mighty God, Eternal Father, Prince of Peace" (Isa. 9:6). The Messiah is also co-eternal with God, according to Micah 5:2.

An example of One who is separate and yet identical with God is the Angel of the Lord described in Genesis 22:15-16.[2] This combination of distinctness and identity is also obvious in Isaiah 48:16. In this passage the Lord is the speaker. Yet He refers to the two other Persons of the Godhead by saying, "And now the Lord God has sent Me, and His Spirit."

But the case for the threeness of God is far stronger in the New Testament. There it can be unequivocally shown that the Father is God, the Son is God, and the Holy Spirit is God. The New Testament also teaches that these three names are not synonymous, but speak of three distinct and equal Persons.

The New Testament leaves no doubt that the Father is God. He is called "God the Father" (1 Peter 1:2). The Father's identity as God is also stated by John and Paul (John 6:27; Eph. 4:6).

Jesus Christ is also God. We considered the biblical evidence for this fact in chapter 2. His deity is proven by the divine names given Him, by His works which only God could do, by His divine attributes (eternality, John 17:5; omnipresence, Matt. 28:20; omnipotence, Heb. 1:3; omniscience, Matt. 9:4), and by explicit statements of His deity (John 1:1; 20:28; Titus 2:13).

The Holy Spirit is God. One of the clearest attestations of this fact is found in Acts 5:3-4, where a lie to the Holy Spirit in verse 3 is equated with a lie to God in verse 4. The deity of the Holy Spirit can also be seen in the divine names used of Him (for example, "the Spirit of our God," 1 Cor. 6:11), in His attributes of deity (omnipresence, Ps. 139:7; omnipotence, Job 33:4; omniscience, 1 Cor. 2:10-12), and in His divine works (Gen. 1:2; Luke 1:35; John 3:5-6; 16:8; Rom. 8:26; 2 Tim. 3:16; 2 Peter 1:21):

Thus, the Scriptures teach that God is One and Three. There are a few passages in the New Testament which speak of *all three* members of the Godhead as distinct Persons. One of these is Matthew 3:16-17: Jesus is being baptized, the Spirit of God descends upon Him as a dove, and the Father speaks from heaven.

There is also the threefold benediction at the end of 2 Corinthians which associates the three Persons of God on an equal plane: "The grace of the Lord Jesus Christ, and the love of God, and the fellowship of the Holy Spirit be with you all" (13:14).

The verse which seems best to capture the balance of the Trinity is Matthew 28:19: " . . . baptizing them in the name of the Father and the Son and the Holy Spirit." Notice that the word *name* is singular, indicating the unity of the Godhead. At the same time the threeness of God is also indicated by the list of the three Persons.

Toward a Definition

Here as in other areas of theology the Bible does not give us a formal definition. However, it does provide all the essential elements since it speaks of the distinctions within the unified Godhead and tells how the three Persons are related.

One of the most satisfactory definitions has been given by Warfield: "There is one only and true God, but in the unity of the Godhead there are three coeternal and coequal Persons, the same in substance but distinct in subsistence." [3] The word *substance* speaks of God's essential nature or being, and *subsistence* describes His mode or quality of existence.

However, as good as this definition is, it still falls short of capturing the mystery of the Trinity. For instance, the word *Persons* is somewhat misleading because it implies three separate rational and moral individuals. "But in the being of God there are not three individuals, but only three personal self-distinctions within the one divine essence." [4]

The intellect, emotions, and will of the Three-in-One God are manifested as much in His oneness as they are in His threeness. The Father, Son, and Holy Spirit are distinct in their personhoods, and yet they act and exist as a unit.

Perhaps we should speak of the "three Unipersons" of the Godhead to capture the idea that while there are three personal distinctions, they are nevertheless one God.

So there is an ultimate unity within diversity and an ultimate diversity within unity. God has always been the Three-in-One, since all three of Him have always existed. The existence of the Son and of the Holy Spirit is not a derivative existence. It is an absolute and non-antecedent existence; they do not derive their being from the Father. The living God is the absolute One and Three. He is contained within Himself and He exists because of Himself.[5]

In formulating a picture of the Trinity, we should also note that while the Three are equally divine and eternal, there is nevertheless a strong element of subordination. This subordination is not intrinsic (since no member is inferior to another) but relational. The Scriptures indicate an order of priority or antecedence in the way God operates and reveals Himself.

The Father is especially active as the Originator, Creator, and Sustainer of the universe. Yet this creation of the Father is through the Son and by the Holy Spirit. Similarly, while revelation and redemption are most closely linked with the person and work of Jesus Christ, they are from the Father, through the Son, by the Holy Spirit. The same may be said of the special ministries of the Holy Spirit.

No Clear Solutions

If these attempts at defining and describing the Trinity leave you befuddled, perhaps the forthcoming illustrations will help a bit. But, remember, antinomies are beyond human comprehension, so the Trinity is not going to become completely understandable. You are still going to be left with the antinomy that God is One and Three. The three Persons are mutually exhaustive of one another, and yet they are *not* each other![6] God's Word simply requires us to accept the fact that while the Father, Son, and Holy Spirit are equally, ultimately, and exhaustively God, they are nevertheless distinct from one another.

Figure 1 is a commonly used diagram which visualizes the truth about the triune Godhead in a concise way. Each Person is seen to be God; each Person is also distinct; but God is nevertheless only one God.

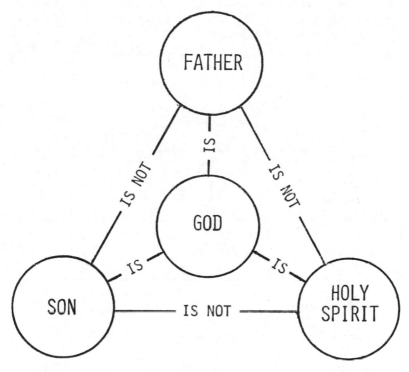

FIGURE 1

Illustrations Help, but They Break Down

There have been many attempts to illustrate the nature of the triune Godhead from the creation and from human experience. It is true that God has revealed things about Himself in nature (Rom. 1:20). It is also true that man is still in the image of God, though fallen. Nevertheless, illustrations from the creation and from the nature of man can never really capture all that the Bible teaches about the Trinity. They cannot capture the biblical concept that each of the Three is *completely* the infinite One.

On the other hand, there are many "three-in-one" parallels which assist in visualizing some aspects of the Trinity. Henry Morris, for instance, describes the physical universe as a "trinity of trinities." [7] Here, the main trinity consists of space, mass-energy (matter), and time. Each of these elements is further divided into another trinity (see fig. 2).

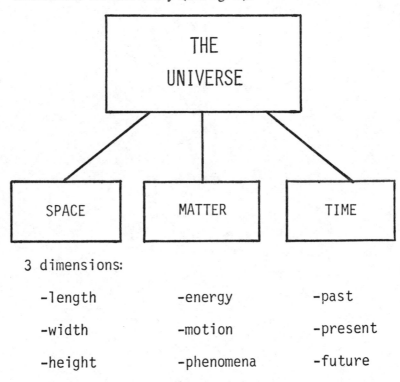

3 dimensions:

-length	-energy	-past
-width	-motion	-present
-height	-phenomena	-future

FIGURE 2

Concerning this space-matter-time universe, Morris writes:

Space is the invisible, omnipresent background, manifest sensibly everywhere and always in mass-energy, interpreted and experienced in time. The analogy is evident when one substitutes in the foregoing sentence, the words "Father," "Son," and "Spirit," for "space," "mass-energy," and "time," respectively.[8]

This is a helpful illustration, but it eventually comes short of the mark. Neither space, time, nor mass-energy can individually be said to exhaust the qualities of the universe. Three-dimensional space alone is not the universe. Similarly, the universe is more than time alone and mass-energy alone.

Another "three-in-one" illustration is water (H_2O). Water retains its chemical identity whether in the solid, gas, or liquid state. Given the proper temperature and pressure, there is also a *triple point* for H_2O. This is a condition under which ice, steam, and liquid water can coexist in equilibrium. The three phases are all H_2O, but they are distinct from one another.

Many actions can also be broken down into three basics: source, manifestation, and meaning (or, cause, events, consequence). Two of these are moral actions (motive, act, consequences) and seeing (the object seen, the act of vision, the mental interpretation).

The idea of three-in-one is not foreign to the experience of men since nature appears to have many "trinities." These may be vague shadows of the ultimate tri-unity of God. Though the doctrine of the triune Godhead is far more enigmatic than any of these illustrations, it should be clear that it is not a primitive, foolish, or irrational doctrine. Instead, it is the subtle and profound product of a higher rationality and being.

The Three Choices

As in the case of the God-man antinomy, there are three basic responses a person can make concerning the biblical idea of the Trinity. First, he can ignore it or reject it as incompatible with human reason. Second, he can attempt to reduce it to the human level by gravitating toward either extreme (God is One, God is Three). Third, he can accept it completely by holding both concepts in a proper balance. In this case, he accepts by faith all the data of God's Word as true even though it sometimes goes beyond his own understanding.

The one who responds to this antinomy in either the first or the second way has literally taken the place of God by making his own mind the ultimate criterion for truth. For him, the Bible is true only insofar as he approves it. Those things which seem reasonable are true, and whatever he cannot comprehend must be denied.

The Two Extremes

In an effort to water down the doctrine of the triune God, many have fallen into error. One such error is unitarianism. This view regards God as only one Person. Since, for most, this Person is God the Father, Jesus Christ and the Holy Spirit are stripped of Their genuine deity. Jesus is reduced to a mere man ("the humble teacher from Nazareth"), and the Holy Spirit is turned into an impersonal force or fluid which emanates from God. The Unitarian-Universalist Church is an example of this extreme.

Jehovah's Witnesses are essentially unitarian because they deny the deity of Jesus Christ and view the Holy Spirit as an impersonal force.[9] This new Arianism repudiates the Trinity because it holds it to be unreasonable.

The second extreme is tritheism. This is a variation of polytheism because the Father, Son, and Holy Spirit are regarded as three separate Gods. Sometimes this is carried a step further into the idea that there are many different gods, some perhaps associated with other worlds or realms. Mormonism is an example of tritheism, for it speaks of the Father, the Son, and the Holy Spirit as three distinct Gods.[10]

The only way to avoid these extremes is to accept all the biblical facts in a balanced way. The Trinity cannot be comprehended by the human mind because it is superrational. Nevertheless, when anyone places his faith in God and the truth of His Word, he finds a satisfaction in this and other difficult areas of revealed truth. There is no need for a continual struggle.

Implications of the Trinity Antinomy

The nature of the triune Godhead has many practical implications for Christians. The Trinity provides solutions for some of the dilemmas which have plagued men for centuries. This doctrine also relates directly to the critical issues of revelation, prayer, redemption, and fellowship.

1. *Antinomies are related to one another.* The Trinity and God-man antinomies are so closely connected that, as mentioned above, an error concerning one leads to an error concerning the other. The fact that God the Son became an incarnated man without losing His deity profoundly affects the Trinity.

Other doctrines, such as the decree of God, the eternal generation of the Son, and the procession of the Holy Spirit, are also affiliated with the nature of the Trinity. And in a broader sense, the Trinity is directly connected with the antinomies concerning immanence versus transcendence, omnipresence versus localization, time, the resurrection body, and divine sovereignty versus human responsibility. Because all things owe their existence to the One who "calls into being that which does not exist" (Rom. 4:17), we might expect all these things to be interrelated. "For from Him and through Him and to Him are all things" (Rom. 11:36).

2. *The Trinity antinomy is an absolute for unity and diversity.* Within the Godhead, unity is no more fundamental than diversity and diversity is no more fundamental than unity. God Himself is the eternal One and Three. Thus, the biblical revelation of the triune God contains the answer to the ancient philosophical problem of the one and the many.

The question that men have been unable to answer apart from the Scriptures is, "What gives meaning to the particulars in the universe?" The Bible tells us that because God is eternally One and Three, He is the Absolute who unifies and gives meaning to the infinite variety of the created universe. The universe is not a chaotic product of time and chance. Instead, it is orderly, harmonious, and systematic. God's own diversity is reflected in the diversity of life in the creation.

The God of the Bible is the answer to the problem of the absolutes and the universals. Apart from Him nothing in the universe would have any real significance. Everything would be relative to everything else in an existence which has no ultimate meaning.

3. *Uniqueness of the Trinity.* The biblical doctrine of the infinite, personal, triune Godhead is unique. There are many, however, who do not want to accept this, thinking that other religions also have their "trinities." This is usually part of a syncretistic effort to support the notion that all religions are variations of the same thing.

Representatives of this view often point to a trinity of gods in Hinduism known as *Trimurti*. The first god is "the Creator" (Brahmā), the second is "the Preserver" (Vishnu), and the third is "the Destroyer" (Shiva). But the major similarity this triad of gods has to the biblical Trinity is the element of threeness.[11] Otherwise, they are quite different.

The same can be said of other triads of gods, for instance, the

Egyptian gods Osiris, Isis, and Horus. They are simply three gods which are related. In both Hinduism and the Egyptian pantheon there are many other gods as well. The God of the Bible remains completely unique as the infinite and personal Creator who eternally subsists as the Three-in-One.

4. *Redemption and the triune God.* In the Scriptures, God reveals His plan of bringing salvation to men. This entire plan of redemption hinges on the nature of the triune Godhead, for the two doctrines stand or fall together. Apart from the Trinity it is inconceivable that the one true God could become a true man, be put to death, and raise Himself from the dead.

All three members of the Godhead play critical roles in making our redemption from sin possible. It is the love of the Father which prompted Him to send His only begotten Son into the world so that we might live through Him (see 1 John 4:9-10). It is Christ's love for sinners and His obedience to the righteous will of His Father which led Him to die as our substitute. And it is the loving ministry of the Holy Spirit which applies the benefits of the blood of Christ to all who want God's free gift of eternal life.

It follows that those who deny the Trinity must also have a poor view of Jesus Christ, the Holy Spirit, and the nature of salvation.

5. *The ultimate fellowship.* The fact that God is a perfect Trinity means that in Him is all the fullness of being, life, and fellowship. God is living love, self-conscious and dynamic.

Love is impossible without a lover and a beloved. Within the triune Godhead there is a perfect interrelationship of love, lover, and beloved. God can indeed rejoice in Himself.

This mutual intimacy within the Godhead is clearly seen in Christ's high priestly prayer: "And now, glorify Thou Me together with Thyself, Father, with the glory which I ever had with Thee before the world was. . . . Thou didst love Me before the foundation of the world" (John 17:5, 24).

Because God has perfect fellowship and love within His own being, absolutes for fellowship and love exist. And because God created us in His image, we can have true fellowship with God and with one another. God's love for us makes all this possible: "And the glory which Thou hast given Me I have given to them; that they may be one, just as We are one; I in them, and Thou in Me, that they may be perfected in unity, that the world may know that Thou didst send Me, and didst love them, even as Thou didst love Me" (John 17:22-23).

Fellowship and love, then, are based completely on the fact that God is a Tri-unity.

When the church is made complete at the resurrection, it will reflect the personal unity and diversity within the Godhead. Perfect fellowship will exist not only among the members of the body of Christ but also between the body of Christ and the living God. The fellowship that we can now enjoy with God and other men is a pale reflection of what God holds in store for those who know Jesus Christ.

6. *Revelation, prayer, and the Trinity.* God's revelation of Himself to man is also based on the nature of the Trinity. "As God can, in an absolute sense, communicate Himself inwards in an act of self-revelation among the three Persons, so He is able, in a relative sense, to impart Himself outwards in revelation and communication to His creation." [12]

Even the way we approach God in prayer is dependent on the Trinity. In prayer, the Holy Spirit intercedes for us, for we do not know how to pray as we should (Rom. 8:26). The Father is the One to whom we pray, but we must pray in the name of the Son (see John 16:23-24).

Though we cannot comprehend the biblical doctrine of the Trinity, the things God has chosen to reveal about His Three-in-One nature are extremely important. The doctrine of the Trinity connects closely with other important doctrines, including the work of redemption, the God-man, and revelation. This unique biblical teaching invades everything we know about love, fellowship, prayer, and worship.

4 Divine Sovereignty Versus Human Responsibility (Salvation)

Antinomies are forced upon us by the facts of God's Word; we are not inventing them ourselves. Since His written revelation teaches concepts which appear to be mutually exclusive, we must realize that with God both truths are friends, not enemies. In God's higher rationality, things which we think must be either-or can in reality be both-and.

Thus, *when the biblical facts warrant them,* we can embrace the antinomies in the Bible and relate them to the omniscience and omnipotence of God. There is no need to abandon rationality for nonsense as the White Queen does in Lewis Carroll's *Through the Looking-Glass:*

> "I can't believe *that!*" said Alice.
>
> "Can't you?" the Queen said in a pitying tone. "Try again: draw a long breath, and shut your eyes."
>
> Alice laughed. "There's no use trying," she said, "one *can't* believe impossible things."
>
> "I daresay you haven't had much practice," said the Queen. "When I was your age, I always did it for half-an-hour a day. Why, sometimes I've believed as many as six impossible things before breakfast." [1]

Neither do we need to adopt Tertullian's position: "I believe it because it is absurd." Christians should say instead: "I believe it because God says it in the Bible."

The General Problem

God has revealed to us in the Bible that He not only created all things but He also preplanned everything that would happen in His creation. He both knows everything that has happened and everything that is yet future. He actively decreed every detail of this reality, and He is sovereign over all. But here is where the antinomy comes in: even though God is sovereign, man still has real responsibility and freedom in the choices he makes. These choices are his own; he cannot blame God for them. And they will genuinely affect and modify the rest of his life.

Because this antinomy more intimately affects us than most of the others, it is one of the most difficult to accept. When people face it, they tend to overemphasize one truth (God's sovereignty) or the other (human responsibility). This produces a lack of balance.

This antinomy manifests itself in different ways. For instance, it relates to the issue of election and faith in the doctrine of salvation, as we will see later in this chapter. It also relates to the problem of evil, that is, how evil could enter the creation without God being responsible for it. We will examine this age-old problem in chapter 5.

But first we need to demonstrate from the Word of God the truth of the two basic propositions in this antinomy. Do the Scriptures really say that man is completely responsible for what he does even though God planned everything that would come to pass?

Divine Sovereignty

God is able to do anything He desires. "I know that Thou canst do all things, and that no purpose of Thine can be thwarted" (Job 42:2). "Whatever the Lord pleases, He does, in heaven and in earth, in the seas and in all deeps" (Ps. 135:6). The Lord carries out everything exactly as planned.

"Have you not heard? Long ago I did it; from ancient times I planned it. Now I have brought it to pass" (2 Kings 19:25). "God is not a man, that He should lie, nor a son of man, that He should repent; has He said, and will He not do it? Or has He spoken, and will He not make it good?" (Num. 23:19) All that God has preplanned is as good as done. Nothing can change it, for *there is no authority above God.* As He says through Isaiah, "To whom then will you liken Me that I should be his equal?" (Isa. 40:25)

Because of His complete uniqueness and sovereignty, God is able to declare, "I am God, and there is no other: I am God, and there is no one like Me, declaring the end from the beginning and from ancient times things which have not been done, saying, 'My purpose will be established, and I will accomplish all My good pleasure' " (Isa. 46:9-10; see also Isa. 14:24, 27; 43:13).

God directs the history of the universe along the course of His foreordained plan. This involves His ability to choose individuals and groups for special purposes in the outworking of this plan. For instance, Jeremiah and Paul were chosen by God to have special missions even before they were formed in their mothers' wombs (Jer. 1:5; Gal. 1:15).

God also elects individuals for salvation. Christ speaks of those elected for salvation (Matt. 24:22, 24, 31; Luke 18:7), and Paul clearly endorses this concept (Rom. 8:29-33; Col. 3:12; 2 Tim. 2:10; Titus 1:1; see also 1 Peter 1:1-2; 2 John 1).

Ephesians 1:4-5, 11 is particularly striking. God's election of those who would be saved is pretemporal, "before the foundation of the world," according to verse 4. This choice involved love and it was based on God's kindness. "He predestined us to adoption as sons through Jesus Christ to Himself, according to the kind intention of His will" (v. 5).

God's sovereignty is self-determined, and this fact is emphasized three times (vv. 5, 9, 11). In God's loving purpose, all things have been designed to lead "to the praise of His glory" (vv. 6, 12, 14). It is best that God works in all things, for only in this way will all things ultimately glorify God. This glorification is consistent with God's love and kindness because He alone is worthy of ultimate glorification. (Nevertheless, God will also glorify all believers at the resurrection when He finally conforms us to the image of His Son. But even God's act of glorifying others will bring greater glory to Himself.)

God's sovereign purpose extends to all things in His creation and is not limited by space or time. This plan is so complete that Scripture declares, "The lot is cast into the lap, but its every decision is from the Lord" (Prov. 16:33). Consider the implications of a statement like this! Ultimately there is no *chance* in this universe because even the workings of probability and statistics are controlled by God. There are no real accidents and God is surprised by nothing.

We have seen that God's eternal plan is all-inclusive, extending even to His election of those who will be saved.[2]

But what about those not elected for salvation? Most theologians would naturally prefer to limit the bounds of God's sovereign plan at this point. The word *preterition* is often used here, meaning that God "passes by" the non-elect.

However, several passages in Scripture seem to support a more active role on God's part. If this is so, *reprobation* may be a more appropriate word than *preterition*.

Romans 9:10-24 is one passage that should be carefully studied. God has mercy on whom He desires, and He hardens whom He desires—both verbs are active (v. 18). God's choice is not based on human merit, but on His mercy and inscrutable purposes. But if God hardens some, how can human responsibility be real? How can He blame the non-elect for not doing His will? (v. 19) God answers that *the question is out of order* (v. 20). We know that there is no injustice with God (v. 14), and, therefore, as vessels we must trust the Potter. For man this issue is an antinomy.

Another passage along this line is 1 Peter 2:8. Speaking of those who reject Jesus Christ, Peter says that "they stumble because they are disobedient to the Word, *and to this doom they were also appointed.*" Scripture also says, "The Lord has made everything for its own purpose, even the wicked for the day of evil" (Prov. 16:4; also compare Ps. 92:6-7). Other verses also reveal how God hardens hearts (Isa. 6:10; 44:18; John 12:40; Rom. 11:7-8, 25).

Human Responsibility

Just as biblical a doctrine as divine sovereignty is human responsibility. For instance, Romans 9 (God's sovereignty) is not complete without Romans 10 (human responsibility): "For the Scripture says, 'Whoever believes in Him will not be disappointed.' For there is no distinction between Jew and Greek; for the same Lord is Lord of all, abounding in riches for all who call upon Him; for 'Whoever will call upon the name of the Lord will be saved'" (Rom. 10:11-13).

King Saul furnishes a good example of the reality of human responsibility. His disobedience cost him a kingdom which would have been everlasting—"the Lord would have established your kingdom over Israel forever" (1 Sam. 13:13). God later said of Saul, "I regret that I have made Saul king, for he has turned back from following Me, and has not carried out My commands" (1 Sam. 15:11).

The Bible makes it clear that we are not pawns in the hands of a deterministic and fatalistic universe. Every command in the Old and New Testaments is proof of the reality of human responsibility from God's perspective.

A number of passages neatly juxtapose the truths of God's complete sovereignty and man's responsibility. Consider, for instance, the crucifixion of the Son of God. Men were responsible for putting Jesus to death even though He was "delivered up by the predetermined plan and foreknowledge of God" (Acts 2:23). Those who were gathered together against Jesus simply did what God's hand and God's purpose predestined to occur, according to Acts 4:27-28. This antinomy also relates directly to Judas Iscariot and his betrayal of Christ: "For indeed, the Son of Man is going *as it has been determined;* but woe to that man through whom He is betrayed!" (Luke 22:22)

God is the divine Potter who has "a right over the clay, to make from the same lump one vessel for honorable use, and another for common use" according to His own purpose (Rom. 9:21). Yet this "clay" has a will and is responsible for the choices it freely makes. (Read Jeremiah 18:1-12 to see how the prophet subtly intertwines these antinomial concepts.)

God is omniscient. Even when He "changes His mind" (as in Jer. 18:8, 10), it is because He had planned to do so from eternity. In His omniscience He also knew the Jews would not turn back from their sins (indeed, He had even hardened their hearts; Isa. 63:17). Yet His appeal to Judah was no sham (Jer. 18:11); it was a valid offer. Another Old Testament passage which combines the two themes of God's control and man's responsibility is Isaiah 63:15—64:12 with 65:1-2.

Philippians 2:12-13 is a very practical passage in which we may observe a perfect balance of these two truths. Paul is talking about the outworking of the Christian life. He emphasizes the aspect of human responsibility in this process (v. 12), and he also emphasizes God's sovereign control (v. 13). God is controlling and man is responsible. Neither of these two verses should be quoted without the other, because the Bible keeps both truths in perfect balance.

Synthesis of Divine Sovereignty and Human Responsibility

God is the supreme Ruler over this universe which He created. His plan affects every detail of this creation. This plan is eternal, and there never was another plan. Thus, terms like purpose, foreknowledge, predestination, and election are logically related; and they are equally timeless (see chap. 7).

God's complete control over His creation is based on His omniscience and omnipotence. Since God has a knowledge of all things actual and possible, His eternal plan is not based upon blind choice. Instead, God has wisely chosen a plan in which all details will finally work together to bring about the greatest good (the glorification of God). Since God is the absolute of truth, goodness, and love, His plan is a reflection of His own being and nature.

Not only has God chosen the best possible plan; He also has the power and authority to bring it about (omnipotence). When God promises to do something, there is no question that it will be done. This is why every biblical prophecy will be perfectly fulfilled.

Nevertheless, God carries out His all-inclusive plan by a variety of means. God may directly intervene or He may achieve His purpose by an indirect agency (e.g., the laws of nature). He may even fulfill His plan by taking His hands off in a given situation (the phrase "God gave them over" appears three times in Rom. 1:24-28). But God is in control regardless of what means He chooses to use.

The Bible makes it clear that God's work in predestination and election is loving (Eph. 1:4-5; 1 John 4:7), wise (Rom. 11:33; 16:27), and just (Gen. 18:25; Rom. 3:4-6). "The Lord is righteous in all His ways, and kind in all His deeds" (Ps. 145:17).

In some inexplicable way God has seen fit to incorporate human freedom and responsibility into His all-inclusive plan. Even though the Lord is in sovereign control of the details in His creation, He never forces any man to do anything against his will. The fact that He judges sin means that He is not responsible for the commission of the sins He judges. When a person sins it is because he has freely chosen to do so. Similarly, when someone is confronted with the terms of the Gospel, he can freely choose to accept or reject Christ's offer of forgiveness of sins. Because it is a free choice, he will be held responsible for the decision he makes (see John 12:48).

In biblical terms, this whole antinomy can be summed up by saying that God is both King and Judge. "Scripture teaches that, as King, He orders and controls all things, human actions among them, in accordance with His own eternal purpose. Scripture also teaches that, as Judge, He holds every man responsible for the choices he makes and the courses of action he pursues." [3]

Finally, *God's plan is not always the same as His desires.* Although His plan controls what men will be, the product often is not what He desires. This is partly because God has chosen to allow human will to operate. For instance, God "desires all men to be saved and to come to the knowledge of the truth" (1 Tim. 2:4; see also 2 Peter 3:9). Yet He has not elected all men ("those who were chosen obtained it, and the rest were hardened," Rom. 11:7).

Thus, God's plan and desires are two different aspects of His will. He has revealed His desires (what men *ought* to do), but His plan for what specific men *will* do has for the most part been hidden. This is almost an antinomy within an antinomy, because there is no way we can conceive of how these two aspects of God's will relate together in His mind.

Illustrations

J. I. Packer captures the essence of this antinomy when he writes, "Man is a responsible moral agent, though he is *also* divinely controlled; man is divinely controlled, though he is *also* a responsible moral agent." [4] Many have attempted to illustrate the interrelation of these two truths, but because this is an antinomy, their attempts have proved inadequate.

All too often, people try to apply illustrations of foreknowledge to predestination and election. For instance, they may compare God with a man standing on top of a mountain, looking down at a road which curves around the base of the mountain. The man can see into the future because he knows which cars will pass by one another before they become visible to each other. But God's plan involves more than foreknowledge. Foreknowledge is passive, but divine control is active.

Another illustration involves a person engineering a situation in such a way that it creates a desire in another person to make a certain decision. Courtship is an example. When a man wants a woman to become his wife, he designs his courtship in such a way that she will respond with a willing yes when he proposes. He plans the situation and perhaps knows she will accept his proposal; yet she has a free choice to accept or reject. But even this illustration breaks down. It implies that when we sin, God seduced us in this direction. But that simply is not so (see chap. 5).

The Alternatives and the Extremes

As with other biblical antinomies, three alternatives are possible. One can accept the antinomy, reject it as untrue, or rationalize it. To rationalize it, one must overemphasize one truth and minimize the other, and this leads to the two extremes.

The correct approach is to learn to live with the antinomy by accepting both truths involved because of the authority of God's Word. This means that the principles should be regarded as *apparent* contradictions and not ultimate contradictions. God's revelation in the Bible is always self-consistent. The only problem is that human understanding is sometimes deficient. If we could raise our thoughts to the level of God's thoughts, there would be no antinomies!

But because so many people refuse to let God be wiser than men, they insist on rationalizing the principles of the divine sovereignty/human responsibility antinomy. Some are exclusively concerned with the former, others with the latter. Either error can lead to very practical problems. Those hung up on human responsibility may overemphasize methods and develop guilt feelings about not witnessing to everyone they meet. Their counterparts may minimize missions and evangelism, saying, "Why bother? The elect are going to get saved anyway."

Prayer also depends on balancing both principles. If God is not sovereign, there is no point in praying because He is unable to answer most prayers. And if men have no responsibility, there is no point in praying because nothing we ask or do will affect God's plan in the least.

From a practical standpoint, it seems more objectionable for a Christian to overemphasize divine sovereignty and minimize human responsibility than vice versa. Since human responsibility

relates to *our role,* we need to attend to it. God will take care of
His own sovereignty! Yet, either error is harmful, and neither
error needs to be embraced.

Some confuse divine sovereignty with fatalism. Christianity is
not fatalistic, however, because it teaches that human responsibility
is just as real as divine sovereignty. Furthermore, what is behind
fatalism (fate) is not what is behind divine sovereignty (a living,
wise, sinless God).

Another objection which keeps people from accepting this
antinomy is the problem of evil. Many feel that it is an insult to
man's intelligence to assert that all things occur for the best as
the result of a humane providence. If God is sovereign, is He not
the author of the evil which is all about us? This objection is
important, and we will deal with it in the next chapter.

It comes as no surprise that this antinomy has precipitated
heated controversies and extreme viewpoints throughout the course
of church history. One notable example was Augustine's controversy with the Pelagians. Pelagianism emphasized human freedom to the exclusion of divine sovereignty, and this led to a
concept of self-salvation without the need of divine grace.

In recent centuries, the two extreme viewpoints have been ultra-
Calvinism (divine sovereignty carried to pure determinism) and
certain extreme forms of Arminianism (human responsibility
overemphasized).

As mentioned, people often have more problems with this antinomy than with others because it is closer to where we live. But
we should remember that it is really no more antinomial than
the God-man or the Trinity antinomies, which Christians are
more likely to accept.

The Specific Problem of Salvation

The general divine sovereignty/human responsibility antinomy
can be applied in a specific way to the nature of salvation. From
the standpoint of God's sovereignty, a man is saved because he
is elected by God (chosen for salvation). But from the standpoint of man's responsible freedom, a man is elected because he
receives Christ.

The first truth finds support in a number of biblical passages.
For instance, the Apostle Paul writes of the power of God "who
has saved us, and called us with a holy calling, not according

to our works, but according to His own purpose and grace which was granted us in Christ Jesus from all eternity" (2 Tim. 1:9).

Paul also wrote, "For whom He foreknew, He also predestined to become conformed to the image of His Son, that He might be the first-born among many brethren; and whom He predestined, these He also called; and whom He called, these He also justified; and whom He justified, these He also glorified" (Rom. 8:29-30).[5]

It is clear that in His sovereign grace, God took the initiative.

> We are not to think of Jesus Christ as a Third Party wresting salvation for us from a God unwilling to save. No. The initiative was with God Himself. "God was in Christ reconciling the world unto Himself." Precisely *how* He can have been in Christ while He made Christ to be sin for us, I cannot explain, but the same apostle states both truths in the same paragraph. And we must accept this paradox along with the equally baffling paradox that Jesus of Nazareth was both God and Man, and yet One Person. If there was a paradox in His person, it is not surprising that we find one in His work as well.[6]

Because God is sovereign in salvation, none of us can say that we saved ourselves; this is God's work (see Eph. 2:8-9; Titus 3:5).

Nevertheless, the second truth still holds: a man is elected because he receives Christ (remember that we are speaking of election as an eternal or timeless event). No one can be saved without willingly trusting in Christ for the forgiveness of sins.

" 'Sirs, what must I do to be saved?' And they said, 'Believe in the Lord Jesus, and you shall be saved' " (Acts 16:30-31).

"He who believes in the Son has eternal life; but he who does not obey the Son shall not see life, but the wrath of God abides on him" (John 3:36).

The words *believe* and *faith* are active, not passive terms in the Bible. Believing in Christ is equivalent to receiving Him: "But as many as received Him, to them He gave the right to become children of God, even to those who believe in His name" (John 1:12).[7]

The two truths of this antinomy (one believes because he is elect and he is elect because he believes) are sometimes side by side in the same passage. John 6 is an example. Divine sovereignty is emphasized in verses 37, 44, and 65: "No one can come to Me, unless the Father who sent Me draws him" (v. 44). Human responsibility is emphasized in verses 29, 35, 40, and 47: "For this is the will of My Father, that every one who beholds the Son, and believes in Him, may have eternal life" (v. 40).

Thus, the biblical doctrine of salvation perfectly combines divine sovereignty and human responsibility. God must call and men must respond willingly. This is a unique picture, for only in Christianity is God declared to be the initiator and author of salvation. The only thing a man can do is respond by receiving Christ's free offer.

Because of the sovereignty of God in salvation, everyone who has trusted Christ for the forgiveness of sins can have assurance of his salvation. This certainty comes from the fact that salvation is neither obtained nor maintained by human effort. Since no one deserves it or earns it, eternal life must come by grace through faith. Nevertheless, God will never force anyone to believe in His Son. Free will is still a reality, and all men are responsible for accepting or rejecting the revelation they have received. As wonderful as the gift of salvation is, if God forced it upon everyone, He would eliminate human freedom.

The Special Case of History

History itself is completely bound up in the divine sovereignty/ human responsibility antinomy. Because of it the Christian view of history is unique, since it allows for both determinism and free will. "Both apply, but always in such a way that the evil of history is man's work and the good of history, God's." [8] History itself is both a divine and a human product.

From the divine perspective, "History is not just what happens, but what the living God does." [9] God's relation to history is more than a sequence of interventions; He is always active in usual and unusual ways. God is active in the affairs of all nations and men to bring about His sovereign purpose (see Ps. 33:10-11; Isa. 10:5-15; Dan. 2:21; 4:17; Hab. 1:6).

History, therefore, has a clear goal, and it is moving toward a definite consummation in the second coming and glorious reign of Jesus Christ. Yet at the same time, God has seen fit to give us genuine free will.

The biblical picture of history offers two crucial elements: the goal of the historical process and the reality of free will. No historian who works from an unbiblical base can logically arrive at either of these elements. Without a revelation from the God who created history, no one could uncover the goal of history. We are all minute parts of the process, and it would be presumptuous for any part to think he could step out of the process and objectively comprehend the whole.

Neither can the secular historian avoid the problem of determinism. Apart from a personal God, man is left with a deterministic universe which is driven by forces and laws beyond his control. Only the Bible offers a genuine purpose for history without sacrificing human freedom.

Some Practical Implications of This Antinomy

The divine sovereignty/human responsibility antinomy has implications for almost every aspect of the Christian life.

1. *Evangelism.* The fact that God sovereignly elects those who will be saved in no way eliminates the Christian's responsibility to share the Gospel with those who do not know Christ. God has told us to pray for and witness to non-Christians. It is not our business to guess who are elected, and they are not walking around with special signs.

A realization that God is on the throne can give us a confidence in evangelism which should make us bold, patient, and prayerful. Our job is simply to share the Gospel and pray for non-Christians. The results must be entrusted into God's sovereign hands.

2. *Prayer.* If God controls all things, why pray? The answer, of course, is that God commands us to pray, and we are responsible to be obedient to this command. We are also responsible to meet the conditions for answered prayer (some of these conditions are found in John 15:7; 16:23-24; 1 Peter 3:7, 12; 1 John 5:14). Otherwise, our prayers will be hindered.

Though God is sovereign, the prayers of His children contribute significantly to the outworking of His program. This does not mean that we are pushing buttons, forcing God to answer, for He does not grant all requests. Prayer should instead remind a Christian of his complete dependence upon God for all things. When great things happen, God is the One who should be glorified, not the person who prayed. So at the same time that God is in control of all things, our prayers can and do profoundly shape reality.

3. *The will of God.* God has a plan for every life, but the details of this plan are carried out by the free choices of each person involved. As we said before, however, God's plan is not always the same as His desires. The degree to which God's desires are carried out in His plan for our lives is our responsibility. God, for instance, desires that we come to love Him for who He is and what He done for us. But we are not robots programmed to say, "Praise You! Praise You!" No one can truly love God (or anyone else) without the power to choose.

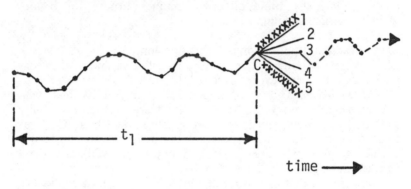

FIGURE 3

Figure 3 represents a portion of an individual's life. As time moves in the direction indicated, he makes many choices (represented by the dots) which affect other choices. At any given decision point (point C), there is a varying number of options or contingencies. The range of options is always limited as indicated by the two lines of x's in the figure. For example, a person who does not wish to be seen has no option to become suddenly invisible or walk through a wall. These possibilities would only be open to someone in a resurrection body (chap. 6).

Our man has just come to point C. He can freely choose among five genuine options. Here is where the wonder comes in: *the five contingencies are real, and yet whatever is done is God's plan.* This is true for all of us. Because the contingencies are real, we remain responsible for the choices we make.

God sees the whole line at once because He is not limited as we are to the temporal sequence of events (chap. 7). Since we cannot see our lines of life as God sees them, no one can live his life as though there were a blueprint in front of him. A Christian should instead place his faith in the Lord Jesus Christ for the decisions of each day. One can be quite sure about what lies in the past (t_1 in the figure, whether a day or 20 years), but there is a reasonable doubt about what lies ahead.

In general, a non-Christian has fewer options at each decision point because without the indwelling Holy Spirit he is not free to choose those things which would be consistent with God's desires for his life (see Rom. 8:8). Until he allows Christ to liberate him, he is a slave to sin (Rom. 6:17-22; 2 Peter 2:19).

4. *The Christian life.* The Christian's walk with God is a divine-human process. God is always at work in the believer to produce the fruit of righteousness and Christlikeness, but the believer is also responsible for acting. It is not a matter of "let go and let God" on the one hand, or of living in the power of the flesh on the other hand.

Paul communicates this balance clearly, "I have been crucified with Christ; and it is no longer I who live, but Christ lives in me; and the life which I now live in the flesh I live by faith in the Son of God, who loved me, and delivered Himself up for me" (Gal. 2:20; also compare Phil. 2:12-13). God is at work in us, but we are also to *act* in obedience.

5. *Security and comfort.* God is on the throne. He is in complete control of all creation. Even though all things are in constant flux, nothing escapes God's constant notice. "The very hairs of your head are all numbered" (Matt. 10:30). Every time a hair falls out, every time you comb your hair, the Lord takes it into account! Here is Christ's application of this truth: "Therefore do not fear" (Matt. 10:31). The fact that God knows you through and through should be a source of great security and comfort. Here is where human responsibility comes in—we respond with trust.

When inexplicable things happen—the untimely death of a loved one, a serious accident—a Christian can find great peace and comfort in the knowledge that a loving God is sovereign in all things.

Next time you are in an airplane try an experiment. Look

down at a city and watch all the tiny cars and houses below. Then meditate on the fact that God intimately knows and cares for all of those people. He is concerned and active in the complex web of their decisions, hopes, and trials.

Each of us is significant because the living God places us in high esteem. "By this the love of God was manifested in us, that God has sent His only begotten Son into the world so that we might live through Him" (1 John 4:9).

6. *"Fate" and "luck."* "The lot is cast into the lap, but its every decision is from the Lord" (Prov. 16:33). In view of the overwhelming scriptural evidence for divine sovereignty, terms like *fate* and *luck* lose their significance. In an ultimate sense, nothing happens by pure chance.

Nevertheless, the biblical doctrine of human responsibility is just as clear, and the lives of all men bear this out. No one can live as though he were a machine programmed by the forces of fate. He must make choices.

7. *The avoidance of responsibility.* We have an ability to contemplate the future and a desire to affect it. The problem is that we want to exercise free will, but we do not want the responsibility that goes with it. Men try to avoid responsibility in a number of ways.

One effort has been to set up a random universe in which the causal agents are time and chance. Atheistic evolutionism is an attempt to kick out the Owner of the universe. If we don't have to answer to a personal Creator there is no need to worry about responsibility for our sinful actions and thoughts.

Another effort in some psychiatric schools of thought is the idea that determinism plays an important role. For instance, "Freudian psychoanalysis turns out to be an archeological expedition back into the past in which a search is made for others on whom to pin the blame for the patient's behavior. The fundamental idea is to find out how others have wronged him." [10] A person's behavior is determined by factors beyond his control (God, religion, parents). But the Bible makes it clear that regardless of the past, no one can blame another for his own bad behavior.

The fatalism of astrology is another deterministic escape hatch. Enthusiasts of astrology desire the power to control their destiny in spite of the fatalism of the system. In a practical sense the fatalism is useful to the extent that it offers an escape from moral responsibility.

In this last section we have considered only a few of the implications of the divine sovereignty/human responsibility antinomy. The biblical truths involved in God's sovereign purpose and control of His universe should lead us to a greater appreciation of God Himself. The more we meditate on these things, the more we can picture His loving concern, wisdom, holiness, and greatness.

5 Divine Sovereignty Versus Human Responsibility (the Problem of Evil)

The Bible teaches that "God is light, and in Him there is no darkness at all" (1 John 1:5). He is the absolute standard of goodness. And as the sovereign Lord, He is both all-knowing and all-powerful.

If these things be true, why is His creation so full of evil? He planned the universe, and He continues to control every detail. Yet the world abounds with destruction and misery. Isn't God the One who is ultimately to blame?

Evil is traditionally divided into two basic types. The first is *natural evil*. There are many evils in the "natural disease-death environment" [1] which are hard to reconcile with the purposes of a loving and omnipotent God. Thousands of lives are lost or ruined because of earthquakes, floods, plagues, and other natural disasters. People all over the world are suffering the agonies of slow and cruel diseases and other organic defects. It is only too easy to find examples of situations which show no intelligent purpose.[2] Nature seems to disregard justice and mercy as it indiscriminately attacks the righteous as well as the wicked.

There is also the whole area of animal pain and suffering. In the natural order, most animals and insects maintain their existence by destroying others. It seems to be simply the survival of the fittest. Does God approve of this might-makes-right environment?

The second type of evil is *moral evil*. By far the greatest evil is man's rebellion against God. According to the Scriptures, the sin of man (defined as anything contrary to the character of God) has devastating results. But couldn't God foresee that man would disobey Him? "If God knew that certain of His creatures were destined to an eternal sentence in hell, we may ask why He created them at all. Is it correct to think of God in some diabolical laboratory dividing people into two groups, rescuing some and rejecting others?"[3]

Moral evil also includes man's cruelty to man. Painful as the physical disease-death environment may be, mental anguish is more fearsome. Totalitarianism, war, greed, jealousy, hatred, and pride cause tremendous anxiety, fear, and insecurity. Sin begets sin in a vicious circle which is constantly spiraling downward.

There is no question that we are directly responsibile for the pain and destruction caused by all forms of moral evil. But in a secondary or ultimate sense, isn't God responsible for planning things this way?

Carnell summarizes the basic ingredients of the problem:

> Either God wants to prevent evil, and He cannot do it; or He can do it and does not want to; or He neither wishes to nor can do it; or He wishes to and can do it. If He has the desire without the power, He is impotent; if He can, but has not the desire, He has a malice which we cannot attribute to Him; if He has neither the power nor the desire, He is both impotent and evil, and consequently not God; if He has the desire and the power, whence then comes evil, or why does He not prevent it?[4]

Inadequate Solutions

The Bible clearly teaches that evil exists though God is omnipotent and good. The question of *how* this can be true is the problem of evil. Many attempts over the years have tried to solve this problem by minimizing God's goodness or omnipotence or by denying the reality of evil. These inadequate solutions have appeared because men are rarely willing to let God's wisdom be greater than theirs. Some may really desire to justify God by defending Him, but in their zeal to help they sometimes water down the truths of the Bible. Others have no desire to defend God. They indignantly point to the problem of evil, attacking the Scriptures with the rhetorical question, "Is *this* your God?"

Here are some of the "solutions" which fall short of solving the problem:

1. *God's goodness is different from man's goodness. God is good in the sense that He exists.* This amounts to redefining the word *good*. It is meaningless to call God good if there is little correspondence between what God is and what man calls good. This view ultimately denies the goodness of God.

2. *All evils are punishments for sin.* This is unsatisfactory for two reasons. First, this would mean that God is unfair in His use of punishment. For instance, the wicked often prosper, while the righteous frequently suffer. The innocent suffer for the crimes of others (e.g., children during wars). "Punishments" are out of proportion to sins committed.

A second flaw in this solution is that it is unbiblical. Christ gave examples of people suffering because of the moral evil of another (Luke 13:1-3) and because of natural evil (vv. 4-5). Concerning the latter, the Lord says, "Do you suppose that those 18 on whom the tower in Siloam fell and killed them, were worse culprits than all the men who live in Jerusalem? I tell you, no, but, unless you repent, you will all likewise perish" (also see John 9:1-3).

3. *God is somehow "beyond" good and evil. He created both.* This is similar to the first solution because it ultimately denies that God is good, at least in the ordinary sense of the word.

4. *The problem of evil is exaggerated.* Even if it is, evil still exists. The *quantity* of evil has little to do with the problem. C. S. Lewis correctly argues that no individual suffers the composite of human misery (only Christ did this when He was on the cross, bearing the sins of men). This observation may alleviate the problem but it does not solve it. It is the *quality* of evil's existence in the universe that we must deal with.

5. *Evil is only an illusion.* This is the solution of pantheists. Evil must not be real if God is all and all is God. Christian Science is probably the best known example of this position. This viewpoint forces one to deny the evidence of his senses. But when he does that, what basis does he have left for believing his senses when he reads and hears about the doctrines of Christian Science? Besides, the *illusion* of evil is quite real, and Christian Scientists call this illusion an *evil* which must be fought!

6. *God is struggling against evil but He is not omnipotent.* In this view God is not to blame for evil because He is not

powerful enough to overcome it. God is good, but He is fighting a co-eternal principle or god of evil. This is known as pluralism, because there is more than one ultimate reality. This solution is poor because it removes the assurance that God will ever overcome evil. If God has been unsuccessful after an eternity of struggle, what hope is there for Him to overcome evil in another eternity?

The Divine Sovereignty/Human Responsibility Answer

We have seen that attempts to solve the problem of evil by denying one or more of its ingredients all lead to a dead end. If God is not omnipotent, He is not in control and there is no hope. If God is not good, there is no point in defending Him. And if anyone denies the existence of evil he should also deny the validity of his senses and thoughts.

Only the Bible offers a solution which explains the origin and future overthrow of evil in a universe created by an omnipotent and completely good God. The solution lies within the divine sovereignty/human responsibility antinomy introduced in chapter 4. Even though God is omnipotent and sovereign, He was able to create creatures with *genuine* free will. Thus, the creature could and did willfully rebel against God, and deserves full blame for the evil that resulted. Though God is sovereign, He did not make any creature sin. Everything that originally came from His hands was perfect and sinless.

There is no question that God knew what would happen when He created beings with free will. He knew that Satan and man would introduce evil into a perfect creation as a result of their willful rebellion against their Creator. The real antinomy here is that God incorporated sin and evil in the outworking of His plan without being responsible for its commission.

Failure to believe both truths in this biblical antinomy can lead to one of two basic extremes. The first is that God never expected sin to exist in His creation. But God's eternal plan, which included the sacrifice of His Son on the cross on behalf of sinful men, proves that God preplanned the inclusion of sin. The second extreme is far more common and is a frequent objection by non-Christians to the biblical picture of reality. This is the view which pins the ultimate responsibility for sin on God, sometimes in an attempt to lighten the burden of man's true moral guilt.

This second extreme overemphasizes divine sovereignity to the virtual exclusion of human responsibility. But does divine sovereignty really make God the author of sin? The answer is that God is the designer of a plan which included sin, but He is *never* responsible for committing the sin. We need to distinguish design from execution. Evil is caused by the free acts of God's creatures, not by God Himself. "God is the author of the author of sin, but He cannot be the author of sin itself, for sin is the result of a rebellion against God. Can God rebel against Himself?" [5]

Even though God does not approve of sin, it is here by His permission. In His omniscience He knew that the plan He chose, even though it included evil, would bring the greatest good.

While God has not seen fit to reveal all His reasons for allowing evil to come into His perfect creation, at least one of them is clear. Because evil now exists, God can show forth the glory of His grace not only as the Creator of all things but also as the Redeemer. The reality of sin made it necessary for God to send His Son to overcome the power of sin and of death. The crucifixion and resurrection of Jesus Christ was the greatest possible display of God's love, mercy, and holiness to men and angels. God chose the plan which would allow Him most completely and effectively to demonstrate the splendor of His attributes.

There are some interesting biblical passages which relate to the problem of evil and how God has permitted it to be a part of His plan. The Lord declares, "I form the light, and create darkness; I make peace, and create evil" (Isa. 45:7, KJV). And, "Shall there be evil in a city, and the Lord hath not done it?" (Amos 3:6, KJV) The words translated *evil* in these verses can also be translated "distress, misery, injury, calamity." God does not create injury or calamity for its own sake, but He uses it as an instrument of righteous judgment.

The Bible never blames God for sin. Instead, the Scriptures teach that whenever sin occurs, God holds the one who commits it responsible. God does not commit evil even though it is under His control. Note two biblical examples.

"Behold, I will raise up evil against you from your own household; I will even take your wives before your eyes, and give them to your companion, and he shall lie with your wives in broad daylight" (2 Sam. 12:11). It would appear at first that God is directly responsible for this evil because He planned it to happen.

But when the sin actually takes place (2 Sam. 16:21-22), Ahithophel and Absalom are the ones who are directly responsible. They committed the sin by their own free choice. God did not force them to do this, and yet He was in control of the situation to use it as a punishment for David's sin.

"For God has put it in their hearts to execute His purpose by having a common purpose, and by giving their kingdom to the beast, until the words of God should be fulfilled" (Rev. 17:17). God is clearly in control, but He is not the agent responsible for committing the sin which results. The other part of the picture is in Revelation 13:2, 7-8.

"When moral agents go too far in dallying with evil, God can so move in their own activity that even demonic acts fall in line to promote God's ultimate purposes. God sets limits on evil and even uses it, but He is not complicit in it." [6]

So God is in sovereign control, but He is also righteous and good. As Paul writes, "But if our unrighteousness demonstrates the righteousness of God, what shall we say? The God who inflicts wrath is not unrighteous, is He? (I am speaking in human terms.) May it never be! For otherwise how will God judge the world?" (Rom. 3:5-6; see also Hab. 1:13; James 1:13; 1 John 1:5). God cannot be a fair judge if He Himself is to blame for sin in the world.

We said earlier that God is the designer or architect of a plan which included sin, though He is never responsible for committing the sin. In a way we can compare Him to an earthly architect who designs a large building or bridge. Depending on the size and nature of the construction, the architect can make a prediction of the approximate number of workers who will be killed. The plans obviously do not call for any casualties, but some will be inevitable if the project is large enough. No one will blame the architect for these deaths even though those who died were following his blueprints.

This illustration may help, but it eventually breaks down. Unlike the architect, God is in sovereign control. But His design is so perfect that He cannot fairly be blamed for evil. Instead, He will be praised forever for His goodness.

So far we have said much about responsibility, but we have omitted something very important. We need to keep in mind that we are speaking about the Creator of the heavens and the earth and all that exists. To whom then is *God* responsible? There are no other gods, and God is answerable to no one but Himself.

"Who has directed the Spirit of the Lord, or as His counselor has informed Him? With whom did He consult and who gave Him understanding? And who taught Him in the path of justice and taught Him knowledge, and informed Him of the way of understanding?" (Isa. 40:13-14) The answer is, no one. No creature has a right to judge the Creator. God's response to the protests of Job makes this point clear: "Will the faultfinder contend with the Almighty? Let him who reproves God answer it" (Job 40:2).

This does not mean that God is a despot who rules His creatures tyrannically without regard for their best interests. Instead, we need to start with what we know of God's character, especially when we reflect upon the problem of suffering and evil. The character of God is the absolute standard for good (see Mark 10:18). It is the changeless criterion for right versus wrong, for righteousness versus sin. This is why sin is best defined as anything contrary to the character of God. There is no antecedent principle of goodness or truth to which God must conform. *He* is the absolute for goodness, beauty, and truth. Therefore, God is free to do the whole counsel of His will, and this will lead, by definition, to the greatest good.

Many have objected to this, claiming that the God of the Bible is not good, at least in terms of the standards of society. But this does not follow since the moral standards of society have no foundation apart from the revelatory base of the Bible. As Pinnock says, "Only belief in God can provide the sound basis in reality for that confidence in the final worth of human life which ethics presupposes." [7] The morals of society should be compared to God's standards, not vice versa. Those who refuse to believe that God is good have no basis for morality at all. C. S. Lewis convincingly argues this point:

> Unless we take our own standard of goodness to be valid in principle (however fallible our particular applications of it) we cannot mean anything by calling waste and cruelty evils. And unless we take our own standard to be something more than ours, to be in fact an objective principle to which we are responding, we cannot regard that standard as valid.

In a word, *unless we allow ultimate reality to be moral, we cannot morally condemn it.* (Italics mine.) [8]

The Origin of Evil: the Two Falls

God did not directly create evil, but He did allow it to be a part of His plan. The first order of creatures made by God were spirit beings, the angels. Nature as we know it did not yet exist since the creation of angels was prior to the creation of the physical universe.

God's creation was good and all His creatures were perfect. But the angels were created with free will, meaning that there was always the genuine possibility of a wrong decision. The angels were not programmed robots, but they were moral beings capable of loving and serving God.

Satan and the angels who fell with him reached a point where they made the choice of preferring themselves to God. This selfishness and pride was the origin of sin and of evil. Many of the angels freely chose to remain faithful to their Creator. The holiness of these angels has been confirmed and they cannot sin.

After Satan's fall he appeared in Eden to tempt man. The second fall, that of man, occurred soon afterward. The two falls are similar because Adam and Eve chose their own way in preference to God's, just as Satan and the other fallen angels had done. The biggest difference between the angelic and human falls is that all the angels were in existence at the time of Satan's sin, while only two humans existed at the time of the second fall. Unlike the angels, mankind was designed to reproduce. And since the parents of humanity became sinners, the entire race would be in need of redemption. "Just as through one man sin entered into the world, and death through sin, and so death spread to all men. . . . For as through the one man's disobedience the many were made sinners" (Rom. 5:12, 19).

Thus, evil originated not with God but with the two falls. This is the only solution to the problem of evil. Nevertheless, there is an important objection to this biblical solution: *"Couldn't God have made creatures who would always have chosen to do right?"*

Some Christians respond by saying no to this question. They argue that free will makes sin inevitable unless God keeps His creatures humble by specially displaying His glory.

Others say that the question is meaningless because it speaks of a different plan and reality. If God is omniscient and omnipotent, this plan (which includes evil) is the only possible plan since it must be the best. Omniscience requires that God knows what plan would be best, and omnipotence requires that God is able to carry out this plan. Only if God is not wholly good could He have chosen a plan other than the best.

On the other hand, this question is not as theoretical as some think. There are two reasons for this: (1) The unfallen angels. Some of God's creatures chose to remain faithful to Him, and they continue to do so. In fact they will remain faithful to God throughout all eternity (see Rev. 5:11-14). Does this mean that they no longer have free will? (2) Resurrected believers will never sin. God will take away their sin nature (the "old man") so that they can be with God and serve Him forever. Will there be no free will in heaven? These two examples make it clear that there can be free will without the necessity of sin. Divine sovereignty will coexist with creaturely freedom for eternity.

If we extend this into the past we can see that God could have kept His creatures from sinning without interfering with their free will. This is precisely what will happen in heaven. This all boils down to the divine sovereignty/human responsibility antinomy. Are we then answering the problem of evil with an antinomy? Yes, because if both divine sovereignty and human responsibility are true (as the Bible affirms), then God *is* all-powerful and completely good even though evil exists. Remember that the truths of an antinomy are not contradictory. They only appear to be that way to human comprehension. What we are offering as the solution to the problem of evil is thus a self-consistent explanation based on the original assumption that God has revealed Himself to man and that revelation is the Bible. A revelation from the highest intelligence can have superrational content.

No matter what God was *able* to do about free will and sin, He is never to blame for the execution of sin if it occurs. As to the question of why God freely chose to include evil in His plan, we must answer that God cannot deny Himself; it *must* be the best possible reality. We will discuss why it was necessary for God to include sin in His plan below.

Another objection to the biblical free will solution is that it only solves the problem of moral evil. What about natural evil? The answer is that this type of evil is also a product of man's rebellion against God. Many biblical passages about the curse clearly reveal that the present disease-death environment is a direct result of the curse due to the fall of man (see Gen. 3:14-19; Rom. 8:18-23; Rev. 22:3). Nature is not now as God desires— it is abnormal. The Bible is *unique* in its teaching that death ought never to have occurred. There was no death before the Genesis 3 curse according to Scripture (Rom. 5:12; 1 Cor. 15:21).

Even animal pain falls under the curse. Before sin entered, there were no carnivorous animals; the animals were all vegetarians (Gen. 1:29-30). When the curse is lifted (partially when Christ reigns on earth and completely at the creation of the new heavens and new earth), the animals will once again become vegetarians (Isa. 11:6-9). Nature itself will be redeemed when God's children are resurrected (Rom. 8:18-23), and this resurrection is made possible because Jesus Christ rose from the dead. Since sin brought the curse of death, when sin is removed, the curse will also be removed.

Thus, to paraphrase Francis Schaeffer, God can be furious with natural and moral evil without being angry with Himself.[9] God did not create man as he now is, for otherwise God would be evil for creating a cruel and sinful creature. Instead, the Bible teaches that man changed just as the fallen angels changed. The uniquely biblical teaching of the two falls is the only real explanation to the problem of evil.

God's Solution for Evil: the Work of Christ

From beginning to end the Bible consistently says that while evil is real, God is nevertheless omnipotent and good. In fact, evil is God's enemy, and He is suffering because of the sin and wickedness that exists in the hearts of men.

God is aware of the troubles and needs of men, and in His love He has done something about them. He sent His own Son to die and bear the payment for the sins of men. Jesus Christ came to face and overcome evil as the sinless God-man (1 John 3:8). Though man brought death through his rebellion, God came to earth to give life, not willing to let sin, disease, and death have the last word. In this way He proved that He loves us (Rom. 5:8; 1 John 4:9-10).

God chose a plan which included the suffering and death of His Son. It is obvious that God was not simply amusing Himself when He created the heavens and earth. But Carnell adds, "The crucifixion, *the worst example of evil,* was not only permitted by God; *it was sovereignly decreed.*" [10] This "worst example of evil" was included in God's plan from before the foundation of the earth, but as in the case of all other evils, God was not responsible for carrying it out. "It could hardly be argued that those who crucified Christ did not sin because God used the crucifixion to save mankind." [11]

Hell in Light of the Greatest Good

The Bible makes it clear that in the future there will be no grayness or neutrality. Heaven and hell are the only options. But the doctrine of hell seems so fantastic that many object to it, saying that a loving and good God cannot send people to an eternal punishment.

Those who wish to avoid the doctrine of eternal punishment usually suggest either that all men will be saved (universalism) or that the rebellious will be annihilated. These are not live options, however, as the testimony of Jesus and the rest of the New Testament proves. Some of the figures the New Testament uses to describe hell are: "eternal punishment" (Matt. 25:46), "where their worm does not die, and the fire is not quenched" (Mark 9:48), "weeping and gnashing of teeth" (Matt. 25:30), "eternal fire" (Matt. 25:41), and "for whom the black darkness has been reserved forever" (Jude 13; see also Matt. 7:13; 2 Thes. 1:9; Rev. 14:11).

Hell is eternal, and this means that evil will continue in some form. As C. S. Lewis says:

> I willingly believe that the damned are, in one sense, suc-
> cessful, rebels to the end; that the doors of hell are locked
> on the *inside.* I do not mean that the ghosts may not *wish* to
> come out of hell, in the vague fashion wherein an envious
> man "wishes" to be happy: but they certainly do not will
> even the first preliminary stages of that self-abandonment
> through which alone the soul can reach any good. They en-
> joy forever the horrible freedom they have demanded, and
> are therefore self-enslaved just as the blessed, forever sub-
> mitting to obedience, become through all eternity more and
> more free.[12]

Because of God's omniscience, omnipotence, and goodness, we can be sure that from all eternity He has worked out that plan which will bring the greatest good. True, it is a plan which cost Him dearly, not only because the sin of His creatures causes God to suffer, but also because Christ paid an infinite purchase price in order to redeem sinful men.

Moses says, "The secret things belong to the Lord our God" (Deut. 29:29). We do not know all of God's purposes for including evil in His plan, but the Bible does indicate some of them. The main purpose for the creation is in order that God might display the riches of His glory to creatures who can willingly respond. Since God is worthy of all blessing, honor, glory, and dominion (Rev. 5:13), the plan that would bring the greatest good for all is the plan that most freely allows God to display and receive glory. And God knew that the best way to reveal the glory of His grace, love, and holiness would be to redeem wicked, hateful, and rebellious creatures from their course of destruction.

Because of Christ's blood, God can transform sinful rebels into the image of His Son perfectly. The crucifixion of the Son of God was the most complete revelation of God's attributes. If evil did not appear, the crucifixion and resurrection would have been unnecessary and there would have been no such thing as redemption. Was it worth all this? Even before God created time, space, and matter, divine omniscience knew what would come to pass.

No one can see the whole picture as God sees it. From our perspective it would appear that many things are out of God's control. But we must place our trust in Him. God has revealed that He is guiding everything toward a glorious and purposeful consummation. When we finally see what He has been doing, *we will be satisfied*. We will learn how divine sovereignty and human responsibility can both be true and there will be no problem of evil.

God's justice will be vindicated, and all creatures will bow to God's holiness (Phil. 2:9-11). No one in hell will call God unfair, and there will be no tears or sorrow in heaven (Rev. 21:4).

God has counted and underwritten the cost of this creation. He is both Creator and Redeemer, and for this He will forever receive all praise (Rev. 4:11; 5:9-10, 12-13).

Some Implications

Most people who complain about evil are doing little about it themselves. Before any of us try to blame God we ought to examine ourselves. We need to acknowledge that *self* is the problem of evil we should really be dealing with. Non-Christians need to turn to Christ for forgiveness of sins, and Christians need to walk by the Spirit and stop serving the flesh (Gal. 5:16). Believers must "grow in the grace and knowledge of our Lord and Saviour Jesus Christ" (2 Peter 3:18). It is interesting that the more a believer grows by the grace of God into Christlikeness, the more he becomes aware of the holiness of God and the sinfulness of sin. The better one knows God, the smaller the problem of evil becomes.

Another personal implication concerns disease, suffering, and death. Christians need to realize that in all things God has a sovereign purpose. There will be many times when we will be tempted to rebel against God because of something that has happened. When things happen to us which seem to be cruel or unfair, we should remember that God has a purpose.

The most important thing is not the situation, but our *response* to the situation. Keep in mind that suffering has a purpose (1 Peter 2:20-21; 4:1), it is not permanent (Rom. 8:18), and it should be expected (1 Peter 4:12-14). We need to keep a divine perspective in order to respond to the events of life properly.

Christ was the ultimate example of innocent suffering, but look at His response: "For you have been called for this purpose, since Christ also suffered for you, leaving you an example for you to follow in His steps, who committed no sin, nor was any deceit found in His mouth; and while being reviled, He did not revile in return; while suffering, He uttered no threats, but kept entrusting Himself to Him who judges righteously" (1 Peter 2:21-23).

6   The Resurrection Body

The Bible gives us a glimpse into eternity to come. One of the significant things about this future eternity is that all of us will receive resurrection bodies. Christ conquered death, and because He was resurrected, *all* men ("both the righteous and the wicked," Acts 24:15; John 5:29) will be resurrected.

Though the Scriptures do not tell us much about this resurrection body, it is evident that its nature is beyond our present comprehension. The biblical descriptions of this body often sound fantastic, and the more we read about it the more it appears that we are dealing with another antinomy.

God has revealed something about the state of His people's future existence in order to strengthen the believer's hope and to show that He plans to redeem the *entire* man. But the revelation is limited because He does not want us continually looking at the clouds and ignoring the work of the present (see Acts 1:11). What He has told us is important because we will have these bodies for all eternity. Our hope for the future should encourage us in the present.

The Resurrection Body
The nature of the resurrection body is a somewhat controversial subject. Many deny that the fleshly body will be resurrected. Some claim that this new body will be entirely spiritual. They use 1 Corinthians 15:44 ("it is raised a spiritual body") and 15:50 ("flesh and blood cannot inherit the kingdom of God") in sup-

port of this view. Confusing the issue is a misunderstanding of *flesh* as it is used in the Bible. Since "the flesh" is intrinsically opposed to the Holy Spirit and vice versa (see Rom. 8:5-8; Gal. 5:17), those who hold this view would say, How can the flesh partake in the resurrection?

What does the Bible teach about the flesh? According to the Old Testament the body of flesh is God-given and ethically neutral. Moses says that before the fall there was nothing wrong with man's flesh (see Gen. 1—2). Man was considered God's "very good" creation, flesh and all. After the fall, the source of sin was said to be in man's heart (the inner, true person), not in his flesh (the outward, visible person). And it was sin in the heart that became visible in the flesh.

The term *flesh* in the New Testament is used a number of ways. Sometimes it refers to the flesh of our bodies (Luke 24:39); sometimes for the whole person, a living being (Acts 2:17); sometimes as a synonym for body (Matt. 26:4); sometimes for our sinful natures (Rom. 8:4; see also 3:20); and sometimes for humanity (1 John 4:2). Only when *flesh* is used to mean our sinful natures is it intrinsically evil. So Scriptures that condemn "the flesh" really have no relevance to the question of bodily resurrection.

The Old Testament is progressive in its revelation of the resurrection body. Job 19:25-27 is one of the earliest passages used to support the resurrection. Though this passage may imply a resurrection in a body of flesh, there are interpretive problems in this text which make it difficult to be sure. The same is true of Psalms 16:9-11 and 17:15.[1]

Isaiah, however, gives a more direct picture of a bodily resurrection as symbolic of the restoration of the nation: "Your dead will live; their corpses will rise. You who lie in the dust, awake and shout for joy, for your dew is as the dew of the dawn, and the earth will give birth to the departed spirits" (26:19).

The clearest Old Testament passage is Daniel 12:2-3: "And many of those who sleep in the dust of the ground will awake, these to everlasting life, but the others to disgrace and everlasting contempt. And those who have insight will shine brightly like the brightness of the expanse of heaven, and those who lead the many to righteousness, like the stars forever and ever." Verse 3 is especially interesting because it suggests a dramatic change in the bodies of the saints. The believer's body will consist of glorified flesh.

This is not only a spiritual but a bodily resurrection, and this whole concept is in direct opposition to Greek thought. The Greeks held that matter is intrinsically evil, a restriction from which the soul must escape. They looked for the immortality of the soul rather than the whole man. The Bible, however, attributes a real dignity to the human body. It is the temple of the Holy Spirit, if one is a Christian, and thus we can glorify God in our bodies.

The Resurrection Body of Jesus Christ

The Scriptures say that the pattern for the believer's resurrection body is the resurrection body of Jesus Christ. "For if we have become united with Him in the likeness of His death, certainly we shall be also in the likeness of His resurrection" (Rom. 6:5).

In writing to the Philippians, Paul makes this point even clearer: "For our citizenship is in heaven, from which also we eagerly wait for a Saviour, the Lord Jesus Christ; who will *transform the body of our humble state into conformity with the body of His glory*" (Phil. 3:20-21).

The Apostle John expresses the same truth: "Beloved, now we are children of God, and it has not appeared as yet what we shall be. We know that, when He appears, we shall be like Him, because we shall see Him just as He is" (1 John 3:2). Therefore, in order to discover the characteristics of our future bodies, we need to look at the characteristics of Christ's risen body.

Christ's resurrection body reflects and bears God's glory. At this time, Christ "alone possesses immortality and dwells in unapproachable light" (1 Tim. 6:16). While some people have been raised from the dead before and since Christ, none of them received resurrection bodies. Lazarus and others were only resuscitated; their bodies were restored to life, but they died again.

Christ is the only one who has permanently conquered the grave by receiving a glorified resurrection body. This is why He is appropriately called "the first fruits" (1 Cor. 15:20, 23) and "the first-born from the dead" (Col. 1:18; Rev. 1:5). Because Christ is the first fruits, we know that the harvest will be in kind.[2]

As we consider the characteristics of Christ's resurrected body, we will see that we are running into facts that we cannot fully comprehend. Somehow, Christ's body is completely substantial and yet glorified. It is identified with His pre-resurrection body, yet different.

A substantial body. We know from the Gospels and Acts that Christ's resurrected body is real and substantial. His body could be handled. Matthew records how His disciples took hold of His feet and worshiped Him (28:9). Christ Himself said, "See My hands and My feet, that it is I Myself; touch Me and see, for a spirit does not have flesh and bones as you see that I have" (Luke 24:39). (The phrase *flesh and bones* has led to some speculation that Jesus' resurrection body does not have blood. But to say He has flesh and bones does not exclude the possibility that His body has blood also. The flesh and bones are the most solid parts of the body, and this is what Jesus referred to in order to prove to the doubting disciples that His body was real.)

The whole narrative in Luke 24:13-32 depicts Jesus as a real person with a physical body. He walked and talked with two disciples on the way to Emmaus and broke bread and gave it to them. Christ took and ate a piece of broiled fish in the disciples' sight (Luke 24:41-43; see also Acts 10:40-41). His body did not *need* the fish (see 1 Cor. 6:13), but He could eat it nonetheless.

Further evidence that Christ's risen body is physical can be seen in John 20:17. He told Mary to stop clinging to Him because He had not yet ascended to the Father. This does not mean that His resurrection body was so glorious that it was untouchable. Instead, He may have meant that "she must cease clinging to Him, trying to keep Him always with her. Jesus is about to ascend to the Father and from then on the fellowship with Him will be of a different sort." [3]

John tells us that Christ breathed on the disciples, and later invited Thomas to touch His hands and side (John 20:22, 27). It is also clear that Christ's body sometimes looked like His earthly body because His disciples recognized Him (see Matt. 28:9, 17).

A glorified body. This is the other side of this antinomy. There are many mysterious qualities which are hard to reconcile with the fact that Christ's body is substantial. For instance, most of those who saw Christ after His resurrection were unable to recognize Him at first. Christ had to say or do something before those to whom He appeared could be certain that it was He. Mary mistook Him for a gardener until He called her by name. The two on the way to Emmaus were with Him for a considerable time before they recognized Him when He broke bread. Evidently the risen Lord could change His form and appearance at will.

It is also clear that Jesus could vanish (Luke 24:31). In addition, He was not limited to space or time because He could teleport Himself, that is, move immediately from place to place by an act of His will. This was marvelously demonstrated by His ascension (Acts 1). Jesus in His risen body could handle objects (Luke 24:30) and yet could be independent of them. We can see this in the way He was able to pass through closed doors when He appeared to the disciples (John 20:19).

We know that Christ's body is perfect and that it is a spiritual body, meaning that it is permeated and empowered by the Holy Spirit. Because of this, Christ's resurrection body is imbued with glorious qualities which He demonstrated before His ascension. It is adapted to the magnificent environment which is yet to come. Therefore what is normal for this body would appear miraculous to any observer today.

The New Testament indicates that Christ was usually invisible, even while on earth prior to the ascension. He only appeared during those 40 days on certain occasions (see Paul's partial list of appearances in 1 Cor. 15:5-8). What this implies is that when Christ is not accommodating His body to mortal sight He cannot be seen unless the observer is himself in a resurrection body.

One last question remains to be raised in this area: Did Jesus' ascension bring about such a change that He ceased to have a glorified body of flesh? This is very important because it is difficult to combine what we know of Christ's risen body before the ascension with the picture we find after His ascension. Christ now dwells "in unapproachable light" (1 Tim. 6:16). This is evident from the awesome though symbolic description which John records in Revelation 1:12-18 and can also be seen in Christ's blinding appearance to Paul on the Damascus Road (Acts 9:1-9).

However, none of this means that the Lord Jesus is no longer in a glorified body of flesh. On the contrary, Christ retained the same form after His ascension: "This Jesus, who has been taken up from you into heaven, will come in just the same way as you have watched Him go into heaven" (Acts 1:11).

Apparently then, Christ willfully held back His true glory and

light while He was in the presence of sinful men on the earth
after the resurrection. No mortal eyes would have been able to
stand the intensity of His glory if He had not done this. He is
still in His resurrection body of glorified flesh as He will forever be.

The Resurrection Body of the Believer

In the not distant future "we shall be like Him" (1 John 3:2).
Every believer will receive a glorified body because of the re-
demptive work of Jesus Christ. Our hope is based on what our
Representative experienced and accomplished.

One of the unique teachings of the Bible is that death was
never meant to be a part of the natural course of events. It is an
unnatural phenomenon brought about by sin. When we are resurrected, we will be delivered from our sin nature, and being
made sinless we will abide with the Lord forever.

First Corinthians 15. The central passage on the bodily resurrection of the believer comes from the pen of the Apostle Paul.
He presents Christ's resurrection as the basis of the believer's
hope of resurrection. He speaks of two representative men, the
first and last Adams. The first Adam (vv. 21-22, 45) brought
death, but the last Adam is the Redeemer who conquers death
and brings life.

Then Paul says,

> But someone will say, "How are the dead raised? And
> with what kind of body do they come?" You fool! That
> which you sow does not come to life unless it dies; and that
> which you sow, you do not sow the body which is to be, but
> a bare grain, perhaps of wheat or of something else. But
> God gives it a body just as He wished, and to each of the
> seeds a body of its own (vv. 35-38).

The Corinthians evidently had a problem with the concept of
a bodily resurrection. The Hellenistic influence was strong, and
led many to doubt the whole idea. The questions Paul asks are
the objections some of the Corinthians were raising (v. 35). Paul
answers by saying that there will be a substantial continuity between the present body and the resurrection body, just as there
is a continuity between a seed and the plant which grows from

it. This is a powerful illustration if you stop to consider the miraculous transformation of a tiny seed into a full-grown plant. In the same way we will be transformed and glorified, and yet we will still be recognizable.

Each person will have his own *unique* resurrection body. The present body is the seed from which the new body will be patterned, but the new bodies will vastly excel our present bodies in an incomprehensible way. The extent to which our resurrected bodies will be similar to our present bodies cannot be clearly discerned from Scripture, so there is no way we can be certain about what will happen to the blind, the lame, and the other maimed people (but see Isa. 35:5-6).

The next section (vv. 39-41) builds upon the previous illustration of how God is able to bring dead bodies to a new and incomparably greater life. Here Paul illustrates from the variety of God's creation His ability to create bodies with different degrees of glory. God can make a variety of bodies suitable to different conditions, and the present creation shows that He is able to transform our earthly bodies into glorified heavenly bodies. Daniel tells us, in fact, that these new bodies will rival the stars themselves in brightness (12:3).

Paul continues the metaphor of the sowing and raising of seed in verses 42-49 with a series of sharp contrasts between the present body and the resurrected body. These are:

1. perishable—imperishable
2. dishonor—glory
3. weakness—power
4. natural—spiritual
5. the first Adam—the last Adam
   (a living soul)   (a life-giving spirit)
6. earthy—heavenly
7. mortal (vv. 53-54)—immortal (vv. 53-54)

Unlike our present bodies, our new bodies will not be frail. They will be characterized by great power and glory while remaining corporeal and substantial. The body will be of flesh but it will not be bound to the earth by its flesh, as we are now.

Many have denied that the resurrection body will be a body of flesh because of what Paul says: "Flesh and blood cannot inherit the kingdom of God; nor does the perishable inherit the imperishable" (v. 50). However, this is a misunderstanding of the term *flesh and blood,* since this term is not used in the Scriptures to refer to the physical body (see Matt. 16:17; Gal. 1:16; Eph. 6:12). Instead, it "denotes the *whole man* in his weak, perishable, corruptible *human nature.*" [4]

As we have seen, Jesus makes it clear that the new body will be a body of flesh, since this was true of His own body (Luke 24:39). The idea here is that our present mortal and corruptible body is not suitable to the future heavenly existence. Our bodies must be transformed into imperishable glorified bodies of flesh in order to fit in the new environment.

The rest of the passage (and also 1 Thes. 4:14-18) describes how the resurrection will be instantaneous when it takes place. It is not a process, and it is not going on today. The "mystery" Paul speaks of (v. 51) is the new revelation that some people will never die at all. Those Christians who are alive when Christ comes for His church will be instantly changed into their immortal bodies. The victory over death, according to Paul, is not deliverance from the body, but redemption of the body.

The goal of the redemptive process. The necessity for the resurrection body is to perfect man in the flesh and to reveal our sonship. When we are glorified, all restrictions will be removed so that we can truly reflect the divine image and thus glorify God.

Two extremes relating to this antinomy must be avoided. One is to say that the new body is the same as the old. This would be mere resuscitation, "warts and all." [5] The Pharisees moved in this direction and brought the doctrine of the bodily resurrection down to a basely material level; they disputed whether a person would rise in exactly the same clothes in which he was buried.[6] The Athenians probably associated this kind of thing with Paul in Acts 17 when he began to speak about the resurrection of the dead.

The second extreme is to say that the new body is entirely different from the old. Many infer that resurrection is a continuation after death in some ethereal spirit existence. As mentioned earlier, the Greeks thought the flesh to be evil and not worthy of resurrection. They hated the idea of the redemption of the body because they did not have the special revelation that the new body would be divested of the limitations caused by *sin.*

The Bible reveals that we will be set free from the conflict of sin when we are in our new bodies. Many religions only offer loss of individual personality (absorption into the animating force) as their "hope." Those who teach reincarnation think of the body as a prison from which the soul needs to be liberated. But the Bible offers forgiveness and future liberation from sin through a redeemed and glorified body, made possible by the death and resurrection of Christ.

Some people deny the bodily resurrection because they fear a conflict with science. They erect ludicrous pictures of a grand chase about the universe to collect the atoms of the departed dead. But the God who created matter and energy, space and time, reveals that He will create resurrection bodies "in a moment, in the twinkling of an eye" (1 Cor. 15:52). These new bodies will belong to a new order of physics.

A summary of features. (1) The resurrection body is a spiritual body, designed to exist in the new heavens and new earth; (2) it consists of glorified flesh; (3) it is a perfect body—it cannot become diseased or die; (4) it will not require sleep; it cannot be fatigued since it is imbued with the power of the Holy Spirit; (5) it will not require food (see 1 Cor. 6:13), but it *can* eat and assimilate food; (6) like the angels (Matt. 22:23-32; Luke 20:35-36), we will neither marry nor be given in marriage (because we will not die, there is no need to reproduce); (7) this body will be recognizable, though to an extent it can change its form and appearance at will; (8) it can move instantly from place to place; (9) it will be brilliant, reflecting God's glory (see Rev. 1:16; Dan. 12:3); (10) it will not be subject to time and space restrictions as now; (11) it will be free from all sin; (12) the ability to appreciate, worship, and understand the things of God will be much increased, because the mind will be freed from the errors and restraints caused by sin; (13) we will be above the angels in God's order (see 1 Cor. 6:3); (14) the body will have supernatural abilities; what is normal to that body would appear miraculous to us now; (15) each new body will be unique and yet the body of Christ will still be a corporate entity, the whole body being resurrected at once; and (16) it can be seen and touched, but it can also vanish or appear at will.

Some Implications

1. *We will understand many things that are now incomprehensible.* The resurrection body, for instance, will be fully explained

only when it is experienced. Until that time, "it has not appeared as yet what we shall be" (1 John 3:2). We do not presently have the categories to relate to the nature of the resurrection body. How could you describe a color to one born blind?

When we are resurrected, many of the things we now must call antinomies will become comprehensible. "In that day you will ask Me no question" (John 16:23). Our minds are now darkened by the presence of sin, but when our sin natures are removed our minds will be free to function more clearly. Our hearts will rejoice in that day.

2. *Our true desires will be fulfilled.* The biblical teaching of the redemption and resurrection of the *whole* man offers the answer to our deepest longings. God is the One who alone can perfectly complete us through the redemptive work of His Son.

Spiritually, our sin natures will be taken away and we will be restored to perfect fellowship with the living God. Augustine declared that "Thou hast formed us for Thyself, and our hearts are restless till they find rest in Thee." When we see God, our restlessness will turn to satisfaction and joy.

Mentally, our ability to comprehend and grasp God's truth will be increased.

Emotionally, our passions will be pure and sinless. Our fellowship and love for God will be reflected in intimate love and complete unity among all believers.

Physically, the troubles and distractions caused by the constant demands of weak and dying bodies will disappear. We will not get tired or diseased, and there will be no need of sleep. It will be unnecessary to spend time traveling from one place to another. We will not have to worry about clothing. As for food, we will no longer have to labor in cultivating, buying, and preparing meals. We won't even have to wash dishes or dispose of garbage and sewage!

Even the little nuisances of life will evidently be gone (for instance, the idea that "if something can go wrong, it will"). The changes will be so far-reaching we will not be ready for such a new level of life until we are resurrected.

3. *We can have real comfort now.* Throughout the Scriptures, the doctrine of the resurrection is used to provide a genuine hope for the future. Now we know God by faith, but then we will know Him face to face. Many of us may suffer now, but then we will

realize that "the sufferings of this present time are not worthy to be compared with the glory that is to be revealed to us" (Rom. 8:18; see 2 Cor. 4:17).

Even though we are now surrounded by the reality of death, we can have peace and comfort in the knowledge that death will soon be swallowed up in victory. By faith believers can say with Paul, "O death, where is your victory? O death, where is your sting?" (1 Cor. 15:55)

4. *We will conquer time and space.* Our experience of time and space will be different when we are in our resurrected bodies. They will no longer be as restrictive as they are now. We will evidently be ageless, and we will have immediate access to all parts of the universe. Man's hopes of exploring the distant mysteries of space will be realized. Time and space—these are the fascinating subjects of our next chapters.

7   Time

Time is a great mystery. All of us interact with it and talk about it, but time is something which defies real definition. It flows along like a silent river carrying with it the movement of events and experiences.

What do clocks and watches really measure? In some ways time is the measure of motion, but in other ways motion seems to measure time. Since everything in our universe is in motion, we must pick something (usually the sun) as a point of reference and measure our time in relation to it.

But time deals with more than events, experiences, and motion. It also relates to different states of being. Each of us has a past, present, and future through which we are constantly changing. And we all share time in common even though we often do not experience the passing of time in the same way. One's experience of how time passes depends on each situation.

Most of us naturally think of time in one dimension, moving in a linear way from past to present to future. This abstraction fits well with most experiences, but many evidences argue that there is more to time than this. Time is a relative thing, and there may be different kinds of time. The whole subject is difficult to approach because human perception of time is faulty and limited.

What does the Bible say about time? This chapter will discuss the biblical teaching on time and how it relates to human history and God. We will discover that God's relationship to time is another antinomy since it is incomprehensible to the human mind.

Time and Physics

Science has become so sophisticated in its techniques and fields of exploration that it has become necessary to break up time and space into smaller and smaller units. Hours were long since broken into minutes and minutes into seconds. But recently even the second became much too large for many purposes. Scientists have now developed laser clocks which can measure pulses of light as short as three/tenths of a trillionth of a second!

But in spite of this technical progress, science has been discovering that the universe is more puzzling and mysterious than we could have ever imagined. For instance, physicists and astronomers are now speculating about quasars and black holes in space-time. They are also working with the problems of antimatter, antiparticles, negative mass, and imaginary mass.

And then there is that strangest of all particles, the neutrino. The neutrino has essentially *no physical properties*. It has no mass, no electric charge, and no magnetic field, and it is not affected by gravitational or electromagnetic fields. Billions of neutrinos constantly stream like a thick rain *right through the earth* as though it were not there.[1]

Even light itself cannot really be comprehended because of its dual nature, consisting of waves and yet particles. Many of the phenomena just mentioned defy definition in terms of substance, space, and time. The more we examine the universe, the more we begin to see what a strange and complex wonderland it is. Consider the greatness of the God who created all this out of nothing and then try to imagine what creation will be like when it is released from its slavery to the Adamic curse.

Traditional concepts of time have also suffered severe wounds at the hands of modern physics. Newton thought that time was something absolute, flowing "equably without relation to anything external." This meant that what we call *now* is not only our now but also the now for the entire universe.[2] Things which occupy the same point in Newton's absolute time are completely simultaneous.

Albert Einstein, however, discarded this idea of absolute time in his special and general theories of relativity. Einstein held that man's sense of time, like his sense of color, is a form of perception. It is therefore subjective and intuitive. We try to objectify time by measuring it with clocks and calendars, but we should remember that all clocks relate to the motion of our solar system. "What we call an hour is actually a measurement in space—an arc of 15 degrees in the apparent daily rotation of the celestial sphere." [3] Time is always dependent on the system of reference.

Time, then, is subjective and relative, but this does not mean that time does not exist. Time is real, and it is definitely affected by gravitational fields and velocity. One of the most fascinating implications of special relativity is that physical processes go slower in objects when they travel at high speeds. Time would actually expand for the person who could somehow travel at velocities close to that of light.

This idea has led to some interesting hypothetical space trips. James Reid, for instance, describes a trip to the star Alpha Centauri.[4] With today's rocket speeds a round trip to this star (about 8.6 light years) would require centuries. If the relativity of time did not hold true, this trip would be too long even if the space craft could travel at or near the speed of light.

But because of relativity, the trip would only take *one month* for the travelers if their ship had a velocity of 99.995% of the speed of light (186,000 miles per second). But during this one-month period, people on earth would have aged about 10 years! Under these conditions time would flow at *two different rates* at the same "time." Thus, the people on the space ship would be time travelers as well as space travelers. In one month they would have journeyed 10 years into the future with respect to earth.

A two-month round trip to the center of our Milky Way Galaxy (made possible by velocities a little closer to the speed of light) would be a journey of 54,000 light years to earthlings. The space-time travelers would return to an earth about 60,000 years older than when they left! If people on earth could somehow view the spacemen on TV, they would have to watch for about a month and a half to get the equivalent of 10 seconds on the space ship. It would take days to detect any movement at all. But from the spacemen's perspective, people on earth would be moving so fast that they would be invisible blurs.

This illustration is particularly interesting when connected with 2 Peter 3:8, which says, "But do not let this one fact escape your notice, beloved, that with the Lord one day is as a thousand years, and a thousand years as one day." In this relativity example, one day with the spacemen is the equivalent of 1,000 years on earth, and 1,000 years on earth is the equivalent of one day with the spacemen. But God is not limited as we are to one time framework or the other. The thing that is impossible to comprehend is how God can move *through both frameworks at once*. This constitutes a genuine antinomy.

We can carry this relativistic time travel idea even further. Imagine a trip to the nearest galaxy, the Andromeda Galaxy, a round trip of about 3,000,000 light years. Even this would be feasible if a ship could move a little closer to the velocity of light than in the previous two examples. When the voyagers returned in a matter of years or even months, the earth would be about 3,000,000 years older!

But what if the ship could actually travel *at* the velocity of light? *Theoretically, time would stand still.* The smallest moment of time for the travelers could be the equivalent of billions of years in the universe. No one really knows what would happen in this case because even relativistic physics may not be sufficient for this. But the implications of such an idea for time, teleportation, and the universe are astounding.

The idea of man traveling at such high speeds isn't as far-fetched as many would think. Reid shows that "if man continues increasing the speed at which he can travel at the same rate as in the past, he will be able to reach the speed of light by the year 2018." [5] This date could even be pushed back to the end of this century.

What would happen if a material object could move *faster* than light? Many say that time would run backward, making time-trips into the past possible. But the idea of going faster than light is a real problem because, according to relativity, "no material object can move with a speed that equals or exceeds the speed of light." [6] One of the reasons for this is that the inertial mass of moving objects increases with speed, and would become infinite at the speed of light.[7] But this does not mean that things having no mass could not exceed this barrier (what would be the "speed" of thought or prayer?).

Some scientists, for example, think that since neutrinos (see p. 87) have no physical properties they may move in their own "time" and possibly even faster than the speed of light.

One final thing about time and physics. Time is not only affected by speed; it is also affected by matter itself. Einstein's general theory of relativity says in effect that matter produces gravitational fields which in turn affect the properties of space and time. Time intervals vary with the gravitational field, so that a clock on the sun would run slightly slower than a clock on earth.

Gravitational fields can even have the effect of *curving* space-time (we will talk about the idea of the curvature of space-time in the next chapter). We can see from this overview of time and physics that the universe we live in is amazingly strange and complicated. All scientists (whether they admit it or not) must exercise faith in believing many things about this creation that are beyond comprehension.[8]

On the other hand, we should remember that the traditional conception of time is still good enough for *most purposes.* Our God-given comprehension of time is very workable. In spite of relativity, the concept of a simultaneous now has meaning to everyone (including Einstein).

Time and Precognition

As we have seen, no matter how much we examine time we cannot really pin it down or keep it clearly in view. It is always there but no one can grasp it. This is why we should not be too hasty to accept conventional views of time.

One such view is that whatever is not *now* (that is, the past and the future) does not exist. Because we see reality in a progressive sequence of nows, we assume that everything is real only when it is now. There are some reasons for modifying this standard notion. One reason is that this is not the way God sees time (we will talk about this shortly). Another reason is the wealth of documented cases of precognition (the ability to see beforehand things that have not yet happened).

It appears that most precognitive dreams have little or nothing to do with the supernatural. Also, such dreams are more common than most people realize. These dreams are almost always vivid, and some of them keep recurring until they are fulfilled. Many of them involve glimpses of trivial events, and most of the rest go to the other extreme, depicting terrible accidents or tragedies. They are often brushed aside in spite of their vividness until they actually come true (usually a short period of time after the dream).

In some of the cases these dreams depict a future that cannot be changed. Even when a person suddenly realizes an event in his dream is about to happen he can do nothing to prevent it.

But in other cases the future as seen in the dream *can* be changed because of the memory of the dream. For example, a man dreamed that he knocked down a boy with his car. Not long afterward he realized as he was driving that he was in the identical situation in his dream. He knew a boy would suddenly appear in the road so he tried to ready himself to avoid him. Then the boy appeared (the same face as in the dream), but the driver was just able to miss him because he had been prepared by the memory of the dream.

In a similar dream, a woman was able to avoid the drowning of her baby in a creek because she remembered a detailed precognitive dream which showed her what would happen under the identical circumstances. In cases like these the future can be seen and changed. Because it can be seen it is not really non-existent, but because it can be changed it is not solidly there. It is like a half-made future.

Montgomery suggests that such examples of precognition and ESP represent a natural faculty which is "no more 'demonic' (or 'angelic'!) than a faculty of lightning calculation or the ability to play the piano by ear." [9] It appears that the future somehow exists even though we have not yet experienced it.

But how are people sometimes able to look through the veil that separates the future from the present? To explain this, different writers have proposed a second or even a third time dimension. To avoid confusion, Priestly calls these dimensions Time One, Time Two, and Time Three.[10] Time One involves our normal experience of a linear past, present, and future. But our minds cannot be completely contained by Time One (consider ESP, precognition, and *déjà vu*). So Time Two (the time of our dreams) is needed. But even Time Two does not explain how people can sometimes change the possibilities revealed in Time Two (the man avoiding the boy, the woman preventing the drowning of her baby). This brings in Time Three, which contains all the alternative possibilities.

It is possible, then, that time, like space, may be multi-dimensional. We just don't know. The only thing we can say with much certainty is that our conventional idea of time is inadequate:

we are more ignorant than we think, for there is so much that we do not know.

If the future and the past exist, they must exist in another kind of time (Time Two or Three). We could not travel into the past because we do not belong there. We did not belong to Time One before we were born, and we do not belong even to our own past as we are now. Nevertheless, it is possible to go into the past or future in the non-chronological times Two or Three (Time One is chronological time). A good example of this is the revelation of future things which the Apostle John received (the Book of Revelation). John saw the future "in the spirit" (Rev. 1:10). He was actively there but not in the ordinary Time One sense. John's revelation covers over 1,000 years of the future (see Rev. 20:4-7, 10-15).

Time and God

How does God relate to time according to the Bible? In this area as in so many others the Bible is far ahead of us. This should not be surprising since it is the revelation of the One who created this whole space-time universe of which we are a part. God's relation to time as seen in the Bible is far removed from any conventional view of time. For instance, Moses pictures this whole creation as only a brief period in God's eyes (Ps. 90:2-6). "For a thousand years in Thy sight are like yesterday when it passes by, or as a watch in the night" (v. 4). This verse is interesting because it equates a period of time in God's sight with more than one period of man's time: "yesterday when it passes by" and "a watch in the night" (3 hours).

It is impossible to describe fully the eternality of God. We can only approach this by means of negatives. Ryrie writes that "God is not bound by the limitations of finitude and He is not bound by the succession of events, which is a necessary part of time." [11] There is only one biblical answer to the old question, "Where did God come from?" The answer is simply that God *always* was and is. He is the ultimate origin of everything we can sense. Time itself is a part of His creation.[12]

Peter tells us more about God's relation to time: "With the Lord one day is as a thousand years, and a thousand years as one day" (2 Peter 3:8). God moves in many time frames at once. We can extend the concept in this verse by saying that a picosecond (trillionth of a second) to God is as a trillion years, and a trillion years as one picosecond.

The ultimate extension is to say that with the Lord an infinitesimal moment is as an eternity, and eternity is as an infinitestimal moment. In some incomprehensible way *God sees each moment as an eternity and yet eternity as a moment.* God is in the *eternal Now;* He is timeless. This is why He revealed Himself to Moses as "I AM WHO I AM" (Ex. 3:14). And Jesus said, "Truly, truly, I say to you, before Abraham was born, I AM" (John 8:58; see 8:24, 28; 18:6; Heb. 13:8).

In God's multidimensional eternity the end is like the beginning. He inhabits all pasts and futures and He is in all nows. "In one unified present glance He comprehends all things from everlasting, and the flutter of a seraph's wing a thousand ages hence is seen by Him now without moving His eyes." [13] Only God can survey time in its entire extension.

God alone is outside of space and time; He created both when He made the universe. All of God's creatures must exist in space and time. As we will see, there is a qualitative difference between eternity as applied to God and to resurrected man. God's eternity is not simply beginningless and endless time.

Some have argued that if God is not bound as humans are to the conditions of time, there is no way to make meaningful statements about Him. One answer to this important objection is that space and time are real to God even though He is not limited to them. God has clearly communicated to His creatures in space and in time. His clearest revelation was the incarnation of His Son. Christ subjected Himself not only to death but also to the human bondage of space and time. God is immanent in space and time, and He is able to see the succession of events in the same way we do. The difference is that He is not bound by that succession.

God is the Lord of time. He is "the King eternal, immortal, invisible" (1 Tim. 1:17). "Jesus Christ is the same yesterday and today, yes and forever" (Heb. 13:8). "His goings forth are from long ago, from the days of eternity" (Micah 5:2). "I am the Alpha and the Omega, the first and the last, the beginning and the end" (Rev. 22:13; see 1:8, 17; 2:8; 21:6; Isa. 44:6).

Not only can God see the length of the ages and the greatness of their duration (see Ecc. 1:3-11), He can also see things afar off as imminent, for instance, the New Testament teaching on the imminence of Christ's return (see Phil. 3:20; 1 Thes. 1:10; James 5:8; 2 Peter 3:8-13; 1 John 2:28; 3:2-3, even though these were written about 1900 years ago). "Lord, Thou hast been our dwelling place in all generations. Before the mountains were born, or Thou didst give birth to the earth and the world, even from everlasting to everlasting, Thou art God" (Ps. 90:1-2).

Time and Other Antinomies

As we have said before, all antinomies ultimately relate together since God is the Creator of all things. The time antinomy, like the others, is only a problem when we try to limit God to our own ideas.

A close connection exists between the time and the divine sovereignty/human responsibility antinomies. It can be illustrated by Martin Gardner's problem: "Is freedom of will no more than an illusion as the current of existence propels us into a future that in some unknown sense already exists? To vary the metaphor, is history a prerecorded motion picture, projected on the four-dimensional screen of our space-time for the amusement or edification of some unimaginable Audience?" [14]

This approach is inadequate because it limits God to our own perspective of one-dimensional linear time. We need to remember that God is outside time as we know it; He created time. Things like divine purpose, election, foreknowledge, and predestination are not temporal. They are eternal. Man can set up only a logical, not a chronological, relationship between these things. These are all part of the *timeless* decree of God. In God's mind *there never was another plan.*

Furthermore, God's plan includes *genuine* free will for men. C. S. Lewis develops this point nicely:

> Time is probably (like perspective) the mode of our perception. There is therefore in reality no question of God's at one point in time (the moment of creation) adapting the material history of the universe in advance to free acts which you or I are to perform at a later point in Time. To Him all the physical events and all the human acts are present in an eternal Now. The liberation of finite wills and the creation of the whole material history of the universe (re-

lated to the acts of those wills in all the necessary complexity) is to Him a single operation. In this sense God did not create the universe long ago but creates it at this minute —at every minute.[15]

There is perfect correlation of God's timeless eternal purpose with its temporal performance. "Everything which takes place in time corresponds exactly to what God purposed in eternity." [16]

The time antinomy also relates to the Trinity and the God-man antinomies. For instance, there is the timeless relationship between the Father and the Son which has been called "the eternal generation of the Son." There is also the mystery of how the Lord could bind Himself to His own created time when He became the incarnated God-man.

Time and History
As we have seen, the Bible reveals that God's relation to time is very different from our own. Unlike God, we are subject to linear time which flows in one direction (Time One). The sum of all our nows makes up history. Lewis has said that every sentence of history is labelled *Now,* and history must be read sentence by sentence. He spoke of "the holy present" because of the presence of God in every Now.[17] Time and history are very real to God since they are a part of His creation. This is why all biblical events are tied in to space-time history.

But from a *naturalistic* point of view, time seems to be running in endless cycles. This is the perspective Solomon temporarily takes: "A generation goes and a generation comes, . . . Also, the sun rises and the sun sets; and hastening to its place it rises there again. . . . All things are wearisome; man is not able to tell it. . . . Is there anything of which one might say, 'See this, it is new'? Already it has existed for ages which were before us" (Ecc. 1:4, 5, 8, 10).

This is precisely the outlook adopted by the Greeks. They thought of time as endlessly moving in a circle. To them time was an enslavement, a curse. Thus, their view of redemption was freedom from this endless circle of time. The New Testament proclamation that God has redeemed man in space and in time was therefore unthinkable to many Greeks.

The religious philosophies of India also developed this idea of cyclic cosmological time. Hinduism carried this out on a terrifying scale. It speaks of a cycle of four recurring ages (Yugas) of decreasing length and virtue.[18] This cycle takes 4,320,000 years, and when it is complete, it is followed by another cycle. One thousand of these cycles equals a day of Brahmā, and another 1,000 makes a night of Brahmā. One Brahmā lives 100 years, so this works out to 300 trillion years. The process never stops. In this picture, life and history are ultimately futile and meaningless.

The biblical view of time and history is in direct contrast to these Greek and Indian concepts of cyclic ages. The Lord has revealed that history is actually moving in a straight line from a beginn'ng to an end. The center of linear time is the resurrection of Jesus Christ. God's program of redemption is connected to a continuous time process which is heading toward a definite climax in history when Christ returns.

Time and Eternity

"He has made everything appropriate in its time. He has also set eternity in their heart" (Ecc. 3:11). Though many have tried to repress it, people have a longing for eternity deep in their hearts. This longing often surfaces in the literature of fantasy. Tolkein's *The Lord of the Rings,* for example, is imbued with a subtle sadness because of the progressive conquest of profane time over sacred time (eternity) in Middle-earth. There is frequent reference in this trilogy to the timeless paradise that has all but disappeared. Only a few snatches remain (for instance, Bilbo's comment about Rivendell: "Time doesn't seem to pass here: it just is").[19] Charles Williams and C. S. Lewis also worked with the idea of time and eternity. Lewis' Narnia has its own time, very different from that on earth. People could spend many years in Narnia only to find when back on earth that no time had passed at all in our time framework.[20]

The desire for eternity is also reflected in the efforts of many people to transcend space and time through mystical and drug experiences.

What does the Bible say about eternity? Is it simply endless time or is it timelessness? Cullmann correctly argues that eternity *for man* is not a state of timelessness.[21] He points out that the New Testament describes a future *in time* for man. Time will not cease, but it will go on and on in such a way that only God will be able to see the entire infinite succession of periods (see Ecc. 3:11b). Time is a part of God's creation and creatures must live in it.

Nevertheless, there will still be some kind of qualitative change between time and eternity. For one thing, we may exist in a different *kind* of time. The one-dimensional line of time that we now normally experience may in eternity be like a plane or a solid. This brings us back to what we were saying before about the idea of three dimensions of space and three dimensions of time (see pp. 91-92).

Another qualitative change between time and eternity will relate to our *experience* of time in our resurrected bodies. We will have a different taste of time and a new quality of life. Time will no longer be able to slowly suck the life out of us. Neither will we experience time as a burden or a constantly limiting thing.

We need to keep in mind that the eternity we have been describing is creaturely eternity, not divine eternity. Cullmann fails to distinguish the two, and this results in his idea that God Himself is bound by the linear succession of moments we know as time.[22] But God's eternity is "absolute, divine, complete, while that of man is partial and derivative." [23] God is not time's servant; He is its Master.

Our experience of the new time of heaven is beyond our present ability to imagine. There will be no particular ages in heaven since the physical aging process will cease. It is possible that experience of duration will be brought closer to God's perspective. For instance, men like Paul and Peter who are present with the Lord may be experiencing this long interval between death and resurrection as only a few moments.

Some Implications for Everyday Life

The most important application of this study of time is our need to develop an *eternal perspective*. We must begin to look at our lives as God sees them, and consider the implications our small allotments of time have for eternity. Most people foolishly act as though they will never die. Moses knew better. During the 38 years the children of Israel wandered aimlessly in the wilderness, an average of almost 90 people died per day. This led Moses to contrast the shortness of man's life and the eternality of God

(Ps. 90:1-6). God is everlasting but man is like the grass which sprouts and then fades away.

Because most people do not have an eternal perspective their values are reversed. Refusing to face questions about eternity, they are hurrying as quickly as they can to oblivion, stopping on their way to build monuments which crumble and are soon forgotten. People are preoccupied with the false god of "success" because they have not learned the wisdom of laying up for themselves "treasures in heaven, where neither moth nor rust destroys, and where thieves do not break in or steal" (Matt. 6:20). They do not realize that there is much more to time than the mere chronological time we now experience (Time One).

Ultimate meaning can only come out of seeing things from God's perspective. There should be a sense of seriousness and responsibility in light of the eternal consequences of life.

An eternal perspective is also of great value when suffering: "For momentary, light affliction is producing for us an eternal weight of glory far beyond all comparison, while we look not at the things which are seen, but at the things which are not seen; for the things which are seen are temporal, but the things which are not seen are eternal" (2 Cor. 4:17-18; see Rom. 8:18).

Christians need to be controlled by the Holy Spirit in the realm of time. The Scriptures clearly relate the proper use of time to *wisdom*. The way one uses his time can mean the difference between wisdom and foolishness. "Therefore be careful how you walk, not as unwise men, but as wise, making the most of your time, because the days are evil. So then do not be foolish, but understand what the will of the Lord is" (Eph. 5:15-17). It is always wise, for instance, to obey the Lord *at once*.

The Bible places a premium on living on a *daily* basis with God. It tells us to focus our attention on the present. "Therefore do not be anxious for tomorrow; for tomorrow will care for itself. Each day has enough trouble of its own" (Matt. 6:34; see 2 Cor. 6:2). The only reality we have is *now*. It is always the now that directly relates to eternity.

This is why it is important for us to appreciate and enjoy the *process of things*. We tend to focus too much on product and not enough on process. Even heaven is a process, not a product. It is a *higher* process filled with perpetual activity without frustration and with complete fulfillment.

Plans and goals can be overemphasized, forcing people to lose appreciation for the present that we are always in. Besides, no one can be sure that (1) he will live long enough to reach his goal, and (2) he will know how to enjoy it if he does attain it.

James recognized the danger of placing plans before daily obedience to the will of God. "Come now, you who say, 'Today or tomorrow, we shall go to such and such a city, and spend a year there and engage in business and make a profit.' Yet you do not know what your life will be like tomorrow. You are just a vapor that appears for a little while and then vanishes away. Instead, you ought to say, 'If the Lord wills, we shall live and also do this or that ' " (James 4:13-15; see James 1:10-11). There is no question that plans and goals are needed. In fact, one reason the average person does not accomplish very much is that he does not plan to. But plans and goals must be placed in the right perspective in submission to the will of God.

Time is so valuable that it must be invested well, not wasted (Prov. 20:13; Eph. 5:15-17). It must be purchased and appropriated, but it cannot be hoarded. When it is lost, it is irretrievable. Thus we need to structure time to use it best. This calls for personal discipline. A good flexible, tailor-made schedule can lead to a strategic use of time.

We also need to develop a sense of urgency (see Rom. 13:11-12; 1 Peter 4:7) because "the coming of the Lord is at hand" (James 5:8). However, we should take care not to become anxious about time. Remember that Christ was never in a hurry to do the will of God. *God has given each of us enough time on this earth to carry out His will for our lives.* At the end of His ministry Christ was able to say, "I glorified Thee on earth, having accomplished the work which Thou hast given Me to do" (John 17:4; see 2 Tim. 4:7). There is no need for a Christian to feel hemmed in by the limitations of time. Consider these words of A. W. Tozer:

> The days of the years of our lives are few, and swifter than a weaver's shuttle. Life is a short and fevered rehearsal for a concert we cannot stay to give. Just when we appear to have attained some proficiency we are forced to lay our instruments down. There is simply not time enough to think, to become, to perform what the constitution of our natures

indicates we are capable of.

How completely satisfying to turn from our limitations to a God who has none. Eternal years lie in His heart. For Him time does not pass, it remains; and those who are in Christ share with Him all the riches of limitless time and endless years. God never hurries. There are no deadlines against which He must work. Only to know this is to quiet our spirits and relax our nerves.[24]

We will be able to abide with the everlasting God forever in a new quality of existence which knows no frustration or boredom. Imagine the things you could accomplish with 10,000 years in a resurrected body which does not fatigue and requires no food or sleep! But as the familiar last stanza of *Amazing Grace* says, the 10,000 years is no time at all compared to eternity:

> When we've been there 10,000 years,
> Bright shining as the sun,
> We've no less days to sing God's praise
> Than when we first begun.

8   Space (The Creation)

God's creation, though temporarily fallen, is exquisite and mysterious. It is filled with mind-boggling phenomena that defy comprehension and description. The more science is able to examine the real nature of things, the more perplexing they become. As man probes into the universe, he becomes increasingly aware that he knows almost nothing at all. The horizon keeps getting more distant as he climbs higher.

Even the things we do "understand" are treasure houses of unlimited information. We are only beginning to realize how subtle and intricate the creation is. Upon examination, a tiny object such as a drop of water can turn into a little universe which can be endlessly explored. And a single living cell is more complex and wonderful than all the machines ever made by man.

This chapter will describe some of the strange qualities of space. It will consider the question of whether the universe is finite or infinite. Against this background it will explore the biblical teaching on God's relation to space, for this is another antinomy.

Space and Physics
Space is bound up with time in a continuum which seems to extend from the infinitesimal toward the infinite. Scientists have thus far been unable to detect a definite limitation in either direction.

Let's look first at submicroscopic space. At this level particles, atoms, and molecules are in continuous violent motion. Heisenberg's Principle of Uncertainty states that the elementary particles which constitute all matter are *blurs* which cannot be focused in space and time. Their locations and velocities cannot both be defined simultaneously.[1] It is impossible to visually conceive what these elementary particles are really like, and yet everything we touch is made of them!

But there is more. These particles are not *things* at all. Like light they behave not only as particles with mass but also as *waves*. This is another antinomy of nature because they are completely two different entities at once. It is meaningless to discuss how much room an electron or proton takes up since they are not solid spheres of matter. An electron can even occupy *two places at the same time!*

Everything is made of atoms, which in turn are reducible to almost completely empty space. Electrons are constantly whirling around the nuclei of atoms at such great distances that if the nucleus of an atom were magnified to one inch in size, the electrons would be over one and a half miles away! All the rest is empty space!

Upon further examination even electrons and the particles which make up the nucleus of an atom turn into waves. So the atom is a practically empty system of super-imposed waves. Barnett concludes that "all matter is made of waves and we live in a world of waves." [2]

If this is not strange enough, we can go one more step in the transmutation of the concrete into the abstract. If the particles which make up matter are wave patterns, what is the medium which carries the waves? Since the waves are movements, what is it that moves? "Short of calling it the grin of the Cheshire Cat, it was named the 'psi field' or 'psi function.'" [3] This is a completely abstract and non-material field, and yet it is responsible for the support of all material things.

The traditional concept of matter is no longer valid. Things that seem solid are really made of pure activity. Matter reduces to energy, and energy to undulations of the unknown. Thus, we live in a world of impossibles and in a universe which is more fantastic than we can hope to imagine.

As we move from submicroscopic space to our own intermediate order of size, things appear to be back under control. Because of the law of large numbers, when trillions of atoms form visible objects, the wild deviations of the atoms cancel out each other. The result is that larger objects are highly predictable and they can be locked into space and time.

But we need to remember that the world of our experiences is really a small raft floating on the wavy sea of the infinitesimal under the mysterious sky of the terrifyingly large. And even our world of tons and miles is constantly bombarded by forms of energy which emanate from the realms of the small and the great. Cosmic rays, x-rays, radio waves, and most waves from radioactive materials continually stream through our bodies as though we were phantoms. Forms of energy wholly unknown to us are passing through space, still transparent to our most sensitive receivers.

Now we turn to cosmic space, the space of the distant stars and galaxies. Newton held that space, like time, is an infinitely large thing that never changes. He believed in absolute space and absolute motion. This concept was challenged by men like Leibnitz, and more recently by the relativistic physics of Einstein. It now appears that space can be affected by the same things that distort time: velocity and gravitation.

At velocities very close to that of light, space actually begins to contract. George Gamow wrote, "If we can imagine objects moving with speeds 50, 90, and 99 percent of light speed, their lengths will be reduced respectively to 86, 45, and 14 percent of their sizes when standing on the ground." [4] Objects shrink in the direction of their own motion, but this contraction is negligible until extraordinary speeds are reached.

Space can be distorted by strong gravitational fields as well as extreme speed. Einstein's gravitational laws point to the idea that space-time is a flexible and plastic continuum. Stars, clusters, galaxies, and supergalaxies produce interlocking patterns of powerful gravitational fields. These fields determine the properties of the space (and time) around them. "Wherever there is matter and motion, the continuum is disturbed. Just as a fish swimming in the sea agitates the water around it, so a star, a comet, or a galaxy distorts the geometry of the space-time through which it moves." [5]

There are no absolute standards in the natural creation. Space is nothing apart from the arrangement of the objects which occupy it. The space-time continuum is determined by gravitational fields, gravitational fields are produced by matter, matter is reducible to waves of energy, and energy consists of sheer, undefinable activity, a very abstract concept.

Motion, too, is a relative thing, and there are no absolutes in nature by which it can be measured. No one knows (or could know) of a point in the universe which does not move at all.

We said before that submicroscopic space is relatively empty. The "material" in an atom takes up less than one trillionth of the atom's volume. Cosmic space is also near-empty. Even in densely packed stellar clusters the stars are so far away from each other that there is practically no chance that two of them will collide.

However, the density of stars themselves ranges from near-vacuum (red giants) to unbelievable densities (white dwarfs). The density of a neutron star, for instance, is about *a billion tons per cubic inch!* [6] This is so dense that steel is almost a vacuum in comparison.

Theoretically, far greater densities exist in so-called black holes. These are invisible since the gravity is so great that even light could not escape from the star. The star has been crushed to tiny volume and unimaginable density.

The Origin of Space

Great disagreement exists among scientists as to how the universe got started. One theory of the origin of the universe holds that it had no beginning and that matter is eternal. A variation of this is the Steady State Theory, which proposes that matter is being constantly created near the center of the universe and destroyed at the outer perimeter of space. There are several difficulties with this theory. Two of them are (1) there is no evidence to support it, and (2) it violates the law of conservation of mass and energy.

The Big Bang Theory is currently the most popular. It states that the universe was *suddenly created* 10 to 20 billion years ago. A great glob of superdense energy violently exploded the moment it came into being. This produced hot gas clouds which formed into galaxies and other celestial bodies. These bodies continue to grow more distant from one another as the universe keeps expanding because of the initial big bang.

There are two variations of the Big Bang Theory. One is that gravitational pull may eventually stop the expansion of the galaxies and cause them to rush inward, eventually to form a new glob of superdense energy. In this case a new "big bang" would occur and the process would start over again.[7] One of the problems with this view is that there does not seem to be enough mass to produce the needed gravitational pull to cause the galaxies to stop expanding.

The other variation of the Big Bang Theory is that the universe will continue to expand forever. This variation seems to be more consistent with the cosmological implications of the second law of thermodynamics. The *overall* tendency in all processes is away from concentration of energy and high temperature. Energy is becoming less and less usable, and the disorder (entropy) of the universe is increasing. In other words, the universe eventually will become a cold, vacant, dark, and vast death.

Tracing this process backward leads to the fact that the universe has not always been in existence. Otherwise, it would have run down long ago and no one would be alive today to speak about it.

All man-devised theories of the origin of the universe, including the Big Bang Theory, are inadequate. They cannot explain the origin of the universe. The Big Bang Theory may admit that the universe was suddenly created a finite time ago, but it still leaves unanswered the most important question of all: Where did the initial matter, energy, space, and time come from?

Men without God are constantly trying to answer the old philosophical questions with systems that rule out the supernatural. But all theories which limit themselves to the four-dimensional space-time continuum fall pitifully short of explaining the origin and destiny of the universe and the origin of life. Neither can they explain the complexity of the universe and the personality of man.

Apart from a revelation from the infinite-personal God, there is no hope of finding answers. But God *has* revealed Himself to man in the Bible, and He tells us that He is the Author of all things. "Creation of a universe out of nothing is infinitely beyond anything and everything but an omniscient and omnipotent God." [8]

The Size of the Universe
Neither the microcosmos nor the macrocosmos can really be comprehended by the human mind. Cosmic space is too vast for

any of us to grasp. The best we can do to picture the greatness and the smallness of space is to use our intuition and to work with analogies.

There is no question that the universe is terrifying in its immensity. But the big question that is still being debated is whether space is finite or infinite. Many scientific supporters can be found for either of these positions, and there are a great number of others who say that we simply do not know.

It was hoped that the question could be settled by counting the number of galaxies: If this number increases more slowly than the cube of the distance, space is closed and finite; if it increases more rapidly, space is open and infinite. Edwin Hubble made such a count and concluded that space is a closed sphere with a diameter of approximately 70 billion light years. However, more recent investigations show that Hubble's figures must be revised because of uncertainty about the methods of determining the distances of these remote galaxies.[9] As far as the empirical evidence is concerned, we cannot presently decide whether the universe is finite or infinite.

In any case, space cannot really be comprehended. First, a finite, spherical model of the universe cannot be visualized. If you try to picture a huge sphere, you have two problems: (1) the sphere itself is not solid, and (2) the human mind cannot conceive of a sphere that is *without space outside of the sphere*. In order words, the sphere of space seems to be surrounded by empty space. This is because our minds cannot visualize anything apart from space and time.

Second, the infinite model of the universe is also incomprehensible for two reasons: (1) no man can envision infinite space, and (2) if the universe is infinite, yet another antinomy would be introduced. This new antinomy would be that the universe is spatially infinite, and yet finite with respect to God since it is a part of His creation.

The Bible does not resolve this particular issue. It only tells us that space is finite and puny relative to God. Whether this means that space is finite or infinite in the normal three-dimensional sense is not certain. But relative to the absolute infinitude of God, space is quite limited and even insignificant.

The study of astronomy can be very helpful in a spiritual sense. When someone who studies this field begins to grasp the terrible vastness of the cosmos in brief moments (it is a *feeling* as much as a visualization, and it cannot be maintained for long), he can more effectively increase his appreciation of the greater vastness of God. But the real antinomy of space is that God is outside of space and yet in space at the same time.

Space and God

The Scriptures make it quite clear that God created everything there is by the word of His mouth. This includes space itself. "It is I who made the earth, and created man upon it. I stretched out the heavens with My hands, and I ordained all their host" (Isa. 45:12). "The Lord by wisdom founded the earth; by understanding He established the heavens" (Prov. 3:19; see Prov. 8:22-31; Jer. 10:12).

God "calls into being that which does not exist" (Rom. 4:17). He *spoke* the universe into existence: "The worlds were prepared by the word of God" (Heb. 11:3). "By the word of the Lord the heavens were made, and by the breath of His mouth all their host. . . . For He spoke, and it was done; He commanded, and it stood fast" (Ps. 33:6, 9; compare Gen. 1:3, 6, 9, 11, 14, 20, 24, 26).[10]

God is the Lord over space. He "created the heavens and stretched them out" (Isa. 42:5). Every detail of creation was fashioned by the hand of God. He made the Pleiades and Orion (Amos 5:8) and all the myriads of other stars (Isa. 40:26).

The biblical doctrine of creation is unique, because God created the universe *out of nothing*. There was no antecedent raw material that had always existed. Other creation accounts assume the prior existence of space, time, energy, and matter. Only the God of the Bible is big enough and personal enough to have created the complex universe and personal creatures like men and angels. It is a glorious and subtle creation even though it has been seriously marred by the effects of sin.

As science has only recently discovered, the visible things that God created are really made out of invisible components. "By faith we understand that the worlds were prepared by the word of God, so that what is seen was not made out of things which are visible" (Heb. 11:3).

God not only created the universe; He also sustains every part of it. He is constantly active in upholding all things by the word of His power (Heb. 1:3). All things come *from* God the Father and *through* Jesus Christ, the Lord of creation (1 Cor. 8:6). Christ is "before all things, and in Him all things hold together" (Col. 1:17). We owe our moment-to-moment existence to the Son of God.

God is therefore the Author of the cosmos, and not a character within it. Since He created space-time, it is pointless to try to find Him in the heavens. Could one find Handel himself by searching through the notes and words of his *Messiah?* But even though He is outside of space-time, this does not prevent Him from revealing Himself to men in special ways and in space-time historical events. The clearest example, of course, is the incarnation of Christ.

The four-dimensional space-time continuum is not sufficient to explain the origin of life and the universe. There must be something more. What is needed is another dimension which is beyond nature as we know it. This is a supernatural or spiritual dimension. God is not just quantitatively bigger than the universe He created. His mode of existence is qualitatively different from that of the universe. The heavens and earth are dependent on God, but God is dependent on none but Himself.

Since God is spirit (John 4:24), He is measureless. In the same way, His spirit-creatures (angels) are in another dimension. So it is meaningless to talk about how "large" an angel (or even a soul or a spirit) is. Angels and demons are in a different kind of space which in some sense is all around our three-dimensional space. Spirit-beings are "nearer" to us than most people think. Just as a three-dimensional creature would not be visible to inhabitants of a two-dimensional world, so a being in four spatial dimensions would be invisible in our three-dimensional world.

Even angelic creatures must exist in some kind of space and time. They are not outside of space and time as God is, since they are not omnipresent and they have not always existed.

God alone is the Creator, and He is not a part of His creation. He is the only being who is not limited to space. And yet He is in space in the sense that He is in all places at once. But all places cannot contain Him: "Will God indeed dwell on the earth? Behold, heaven and the highest heaven cannot contain Thee, how much less this house which I have built!" (1 Kings 8:27) "Thus says the Lord, 'Heaven is My throne, and the earth is My footstool. Where then is a house you could build for Me? And where is a place that I may rest? For My hand made all these things, thus all these things came into being,' declares the Lord" (Isa. 66:1-2; see Acts 7:48-50; 17:24).

God is intimate with all His creation and He is Lord over everything He has made: "He is God in heaven above and on earth beneath" (Josh. 2:11). God's relation to His universe is graphically depicted in Psalm 113:5-6: "Who is like the Lord our God, who is enthroned on high, who humbles Himself to behold the things that are in heaven and in the earth?"

The astronomy of the Bible is God-centered, not man-centered. While there are many biblical passages which acknowledge the immeasurable greatness of the universe with its innumerable stars, the Scriptures also emphasize that compared to God, space is nothing Since God is the only Absolute, size is a relative thing. From God's perspective there is really little difference in the size of the smallest microbe and the largest cluster of galaxies.

God has all power over His creation. He will in fact destroy this present universe and create another (see 2 Peter 3:10-13). "For behold, I create new heavens and a new earth; and the former things shall not be remembered or come to mind" (Isa. 65:17; compare Isa. 66:22 and Rev. 21:1). The new universe will be better and more glorious than the present one (Rev. 22:3-5).

Heaven and Hell

Many people have scoffed at the Scriptures because the Bible speaks about the existence of heaven and hell. The current world view is that science has somehow proven that heaven and hell cannot exist. But this is far from the truth. We have already seen how the views of modern science in this area are inadequate because they do not explain the existence of the universe. The mysteries of the universe point to a realm which is beyond nature itself, a supernatural dimension.

Heaven is not "near" or "far" in the ordinary three-dimensional sense of space. It cannot be reached by traveling in any space ship, even if the ship could travel at relativistic speeds. Heaven is indeed a place, but the word *place* in this context must take on a new meaning.[11]

Heaven has its own space and time in which its inhabitants subsist. It is distinct from the heavens of our universe. Paul calls it the "third heaven" (2 Cor. 12:2). The first heaven is our atmosphere and the second heaven is space, the realm of the stars. Solomon also draws a distinction between two kinds of heaven: "Behold, heaven and the highest heaven [literally, 'heaven of heavens'] cannot contain Thee" (1 Kings 8:27). This highest heaven is qualitatively different from the heaven of the stars. Since it is in another dimension, it could in some way be all around us (see Acts 17:27-28). Again, this is not to say that heaven is some kind of transcendent order beyond space and time, for only God can be outside of space and time in an absolute sense.

We have seen that God is planning to create a new heaven and a new earth. The nature of space, time, matter (for instance, transparent gold; Rev. 21:18), and energy will be different in this new universe. It will be imbued with the glory of God. Even the throne of God will be "relocated" since the holy city, the new Jerusalem, will come "down out of heaven from God" (Rev. 21:2, 10).

The Relevance of This Antinomy

The biblical concept of a God so great that He cannot be contained by any space has real significance for all people. Nearly 3,000 years ago David wrote, "When I consider Thy heavens, the work of Thy fingers, the moon and the stars, which Thou hast ordained; what is man, that Thou dost take thought of him? And the son of man, that Thou dost care for him?" (Ps. 8:3-4; see Ps. 144:3-4; Heb. 2:6) Job said almost the same thing: "What is man that Thou dost magnify him, and that Thou art concerned about him?" (Job 7:17)

Man is nothing at all compared to the vastness of God's creation, and yet he is significant in the eyes of the Creator. One of the reasons God created the splendors of the universe was in order to reveal His awesome power and glory to man (see Rom. 1:19-20). The arrogance and pride of so many people is utter foolishness in light of our lilliputian planet and sun. Even our galaxy is only a speck among billions.

Only when one man admits that he is nothing apart from God is he ready to respond to the life-giving offer of reconciliation that Christ provides.

The size of space and God's relation to space are beyond comprehension. The better we realize the vastness of the universe, the greater our conception of God must become.

To admit that there is One who lies beyond us, who exists outside of all our categories, who will not be dismissed with a name, who will not appear before the bar of our reason, nor submit to our curious inquiries: this requires a great deal of humility, more than most of us possess, so we save face by thinking God down to our level, or at least down to where we can manage Him. Yet how He eludes us! For He is everywhere while He is nowhere, for "where" has to do with matter and space, and God is independent of both. He is unaffected by time or motion, is wholly self-dependent and owes nothing to the worlds His hands have made.[12]

But if the earth is so puny, why is God so concerned with all the affairs of our planet? The question that Job and David asked is a real problem because of our natural way of thinking. If you are in a carpeted room, take a look at the carpet and isolate one loop or strand from among all the thousands of similar loops. Now imagine yourself devoting the remainder of your life to the study and analysis of this single loop of threads!

The analogy is not too extreme because there are *far more* galaxies in the universe than there are loops in your carpet, and each of these galaxies contains, on the average, tens of billions of stars like our own sun. Yet God declares that we are of infinite value in His sight. Part of the problem of how this can be so is solved when we remember that sizes mean little to God. Even though the earth is a minute speck in the panorama of God's creation, it is on *this* planet that the central program of God's plan is taking place.

If it seems incredible that God would center His plan on our planet, how much more incredible is it that He would actually send His beloved Son to die in payment for our sins! Jesus Christ created this immense universe with all its billions of galaxies and sextillions of stars, and yet, how He humbled Himself!

> "He was despised and forsaken of men,
> A man of sorrows, and acquainted with grief;
> And like one from whom men hide their face,
> He was despised, and we did not esteem Him.
> Surely our griefs He Himself bore,
> And our sorrows He carried" (Isa. 53:3-4).

The more we perceive the terrifying greatness of the universe, the more we can really begin to appreciate the shame and condescension Christ willingly bore. He loved us enough to become man and pay for our sins with His own blood. "He was in the world, and *the world was made through Him,* and the world did not know Him. He came to His own, and those who were His own did not receive Him. But as many as received Him, to them He gave the right to become children of God, even to those who believe in His name" (John 1:10-12).

9   Space (Omnipresence Versus Localization)

In the last chapter we said that God is outside of space since it is a part of His creation; yet He is also in space at the same time. We said that there is no way we can visualize either infinite space or finite space. Since we are creatures, we are locked into space and time and we are unable to comprehend God's unique relation to the space and time of His created universe.

Now we need to explore another facet of the space antinomy: the revealed fact that God is omnipresent and yet specially localized.

The Omnipresence of God

The omnipresence of God is in itself an antinomy. The Scriptures teach that *the whole of God* is in every place. God actually fills the heavens and the earth (Jer. 23:24). Heaven and the highest heaven belong to God (Deut. 10:14) but they cannot contain Him (1 Kings 8:27; 2 Chron. 2:6). So God fills all spaces, but no space can contain Him.

God's presence in more than one place is incomprehensible to the human mind. David, in a psalm about the omniscience and omnipresence of God declares that "such knowledge is too wonderful for me; it is too high, I cannot attain to it" (Ps. 139:6). He continues:

> Where can I go from Thy Spirit?
> Or where can I flee from Thy presence?

> If I ascend to heaven, Thou art there;
> If I make my bed in Sheol, behold, Thou art there.
> If I take the wings of the dawn,
> If I dwell in the remotest part of the sea,
> Even there Thy hand will lead me,
> And Thy right hand will lay hold of me.
> If I say, "Surely the darkness will overwhelm me,
> And the light around me will be night,"
> Even the darkness is not dark to Thee,
> And the night is as bright as the day.
> Darkness and light are alike to Thee (Ps. 139:7-12).

Since God is in all places, there is no hope of escaping from His complete presence. He is even in Sheol (the abode of the dead, v. 8). "Though they dig into Sheol, from there shall My hand take them; and though they ascend to heaven, from there I will bring them down" (Amos 9:2; see vv. 3-4). God's presence extends to all parts of the sea, the sky, and space. No one can avoid His presence, no matter how fast he is able to travel (Ps. 139:9a). "He is God in heaven above and on earth beneath" (Josh. 2:11; also see Isa. 66:1-2; Acts 7:48-50).

All three members of the Godhead are omnipresent. The Father is omnipresent, and the Son "fills all in all" (Eph. 1:23). Christ declared that "where two or three have gathered together in My name, there I am in their midst" (Matt. 18:20). He also said, "Lo, I am with you always, even to the end of the age" (Matt. 28:20). Christ must be omnipresent in order to uphold all things by the word of His power (Heb. 1:3; see Col. 1:17). The Holy Spirit also is everywhere present ("Where can I go from Thy Spirit?" Ps. 139:7; see 1 Cor. 6:19; Eph. 2:22). All three Persons are present in all places together as one God. There is no place where one Person is present without the other two being there as well.

As we said, the *whole* of God is present in every place. He is not diffused throughout His creation so that only a tiny part of Him is in each place. Instead, "He is wholly present as fully as though He were nowhere else—Father, Son, and Spirit—in every human temple in which He dwells, and in every part of His dominion." [1] He is equally present in all places at all times. Augustine wrote:

You fill the heaven and the earth. Do they therefore contain You? . . . When heaven and earth are filled with You,
into what do You pour that surplus of Yourself which remains over? Or is it not rather the case that You have no
need to be contained by anything? . . . You who fill everything are wholly present in everything which You fill. Or
can we say that, because all things together are unable to
contain You wholly, therefore each thing contains only a
part of You? Does every thing contain the same part? Or
are there different parts for different things in accordance
with the varying sizes of the things? That would mean that
some parts of You could be greater and some smaller than
others. Shall we not rather say this: everywhere You are
present in Your entirety, and no single thing can contain
You in Your entirety? [2]

We must be careful to distinguish the doctrine of the divine
presence from the error of pantheism. Pantheism fails to distinguish the created from the Creator because it says that God is
nature and nature is God.[3] On the other hand, the Bible teaches
that though God is present everywhere, He is not resident in
everything. God fills the heavens and the earth, but the things in
the heavens and the earth shouldn't be called God. When you pick
up a book or lean against a tree you are not touching God as the
pantheist would assert.

The Bible says that God is everywhere, but it also says that
He is separate from the world and the things of the world. God is
immanent within His creation but at the same time transcendent
above it (see chap. 10).

There is no limit to God's presence, and no place is closer to
God than any other place. Size and place mean little to God; they
do not limit Him at all. He does not need to travel, and He can
act in all parts of the universe at once. As God exercises His attributes, all things are affected at the same time. "God is over
all things, under all things; outside all; within but not enclosed;
without but not excluded; above but not raised up; below but not
depressed; wholly above, presiding; wholly beneath, sustaining;
wholly within, filling."[4]

Because God is in all places, He is able to see all things at
once. He not only looks down at the sky; He also looks *up* at it

at the same time. Unlike us, He can see all parts of three-dimensional objects equally well. Imagine, for instance, being able to see the entire surface of a two-foot globe at once. We could only do this by using mirrors or by projecting the globe on a two-dimensional surface (like a map).

The Localized Presence of God

God is *completely* present in all places at once. And yet the Bible makes it equally clear that each member of the Trinity is also localized in specific places. The Lord can somehow manifest His presence in some places in special ways. In some inexplicable manner there is a difference between God's omnipresence and His *manifest* presence.[5]

Let's look first at the specially localized presence of God the Father. The Scriptures teach that God's throne in heaven is the localized center of His dominion. Heaven is indeed a place even though the language used to describe it is usually figurative and anthropomorphic (see chap. 8). The Father, Son, and Holy Spirit are there along with myriads of angels and a host of redeemed men (Heb. 12:22-23). But this place is qualitatively different from our ordinary concept of a place, operating perhaps in a spiritual dimension with a space different from our own. Nevertheless, it constitutes a special localization of God. In fact, the places and things of earth are really only a shadow when they are compared with the deeper reality of heavenly things (Heb. 8:5; 9:23).

God's throne is mentioned in a number of Old and New Testament passages. Isaiah describes his vision of God: "In the year of King Uzziah's death, I saw the Lord sitting on a throne, lofty and exalted, with the train of His robe filling the temple" (Isa. 6:1). God's manifest presence was so intense that Isaiah was instantly aware of his utter sinfulness before the holy God (v. 5).

The Apostle John also recorded his vision: "Immediately I was in the spirit; and behold, a throne was standing in heaven, and One sitting on the throne. And He who was sitting was like a jasper stone and a sardius in appearance; and there was a rainbow around the throne, like an emerald in appearance" (Rev. 4:2-3; other passages which mention heaven and God's throne are: Ps. 103:19-21; Matt. 6:9; Heb. 8:1; 12:2).

The glory of God's presence (the Shekinah) is another example of His special localized presence. From the standpoint of God's omnipresence, Solomon knew that there was no way the temple he had just completed could contain God. "But will God indeed dwell on the earth? Behold, heaven and the highest heaven cannot contain Thee, how much less this house which I have built!" (1 Kings 8:27) God Himself reiterated this same truth later (Isa. 66:1-2).

Yet from the standpoint of God's localized presence, He was actually able to dwell in the most holy place in the temple. The Shekinah glory came and filled the house of the Lord. "And the priests could not enter into the house of the Lord, because the glory of the Lord filled the Lord's house" (2 Chron. 7:2; 1 Kings 8:10-11). This glory of God's manifest presence later departed because of the iniquity of Israel (Ezek. 10:3-4, 18-19; 11:22-23).

Jacob also encountered the localized presence of God. At Bethel he had a vision of God in a dream. "Then Jacob awoke from his sleep and said, 'Surely the Lord is in this place, and I did not know it.' And he was afraid and said, 'How awesome is this place! This is none other than the house of God, and this is the gate of heaven' " (Gen. 28:16-17; see Gen. 15:12).

Jesus Christ Himself is specially localized even though He is omnipresent. Before His incarnation, He localized Himself and appeared to men, sometimes as the Angel of the Lord (see Gen. 16:7-13; 22:15-18; 31:11-13; 48:15-16; Ex. 3:1-6; 13:21; 14:19; Jud. 6:11-23; 13:19-20). He also appeared as a man to Joshua (Josh. 5:13-15).

Christ was localized in a body while He was on earth, and He is still localized in a glorified resurrection body in heaven. Now the God-man is seated "at the right hand of the throne of the Majesty in the heavens" (Heb. 8:1; see Heb. 1:3; 12:2; Col. 3:1).

At His second coming, Christ will appear to all as the glorified God-man. "Behold, He is coming with the clouds, and every eye will see Him" (Rev. 1:7).[6] He will be in one place at one time. Zechariah, for instance, says that "in that day His feet will stand on the Mount of Olives" (Zech. 14:4).

The Holy Spirit, like the Father and the Son, is at once omnipresent and localized. He is in heaven before the throne of God the Father. "Grace to you and peace, from Him who is and who was and who is to come; and from the seven spirits who are before His throne" (Rev. 1:4). "And there were seven lamps of fire burning before the throne, which are the seven spirits of God" (Rev. 4:5; see Rev. 3:1; 5:6; Isa. 11:2). The Holy Spirit is also localized in the sense that the Church, the body of Christ, is a dwelling-place of the Spirit of God (Eph. 2:22).

Selective Indwelling

Even though God fills the heavens and the earth, He does not indwell all things. God indwells believers, but He does *not* indwell unredeemed men. There is a spiritual selectivity.

God the Father indwells those who have trusted Christ: "Jesus answered and said to him, 'If anyone loves Me, he will keep My word; and My Father will love him, and We will come to him, and make Our abode with him' " (John 14:23). Paul also states that the Father indwells every member of the body of Christ: "One God and Father of all who is over all and through all and in all" (Eph. 4:6).

God the Son also indwells Christians. "In that day you shall know that I am in My Father, and you in Me, and I in you" (John 14:20; compare 14:23; 17:23, 26). Paul proclaims, "I have been crucified with Christ; and it is no longer I who lives, but Christ lives in me" (Gal. 2:20). Paul also speaks about "Christ in you, the hope of glory" (Col. 1:27; see Rev. 3:20).

God the Holy Spirit indwells all believers. "However, you are not in the flesh but in the Spirit, if indeed the Spirit of God dwells in you. But if anyone does not have the Spirit of Christ, he does not belong to Him" (Rom. 8:9). "Or do you not know that your body is a temple of the Holy Spirit who is in you, whom you have from God, and that you are not your own?" (1 Cor. 6:19; compare John 14:17; Eph. 2:22)

The members of the Trinity indwell Christians in a way which is similar to the way they indwell one another, and because of this, all believers will eventually have the same kind of perfect unity that exists within the Godhead (John 17:20-23; see 14:10, 20).

To summarize, God is omnipresent in such a way that He is wholly present in all places. Yet He is also localized in special ways. He indwells some people but not all. He is somehow able to manifest His presence in different ways and in different degrees. God's heavenly throne is His ultimate dwelling place and the center of His universal dominion.

Some Applications

The knowledge that God is everywhere present and that He also manifests His presence in localized ways can either be an encouraging or a frightening thing. God's special presence in the garden of Eden, once a cause of fellowship and bliss, became a source of fear to Adam and Eve after they fell into sin. Because of their sin, "the man and his wife hid themselves from the presence of the Lord God among the trees of the garden" (Gen. 3:8).

Jonah's rebellion against God led him to attempt to hide from the presence of God (Jonah 1:3). But all such attempts are futile. David realized that God knows us through and through and that there is no way to escape from His complete presence (Ps. 139:7-8).

The awareness of God's presence can be of real benefit to a Christian. Knowing that God is present can help a believer overcome the temptation to sin. It can also be a source of comfort and assurance, especially in times of stress, anxiety, and affliction. Even Christians who have been long imprisoned for the cause of Christ in some countries are able to find consolation in the awareness of God's presence. Christ is always immediately accessible. (See Ps. 73:21-24, 28.)

One problem that hampers the lives of many Christians today is that God's omnipresence and God's manifest presence are only concepts to them. These truths have a place in their reasoning, but not in their experience. Many of us are like Jacob who said, "Surely the Lord is in this place, and I did not know it" (Gen. 28:16). We need to practice the presence of God in such a way that we live each day with the consciousness that God is always with us. The person who knows Christ can *never* be alone. Our task is to become more spiritually perceptive of God's presence and to become increasingly aware of His nearness.

One way we can do this is through *prayer*. Ask God to make you more sensitive to His presence. Begin to prayerfully regard Him as One who is constantly with you (see 1 Thes. 5:17). Also, study Psalm 139 to learn how David understood and acted on these truths.

10 The Transcendent-Immanent God

The Bible reveals that God is both transcendent and immanent. The transcendence of God means that in His being, God is exalted above and is distinct from the universe.

The immanence of God means that He pervades and sustains the universe. (Be sure to distinguish *immanent* from *imminent*. When something is imminent, it is impending, or, ready to take place.)

When we put these two concepts together, we find that God is at once both near and far. He indwells believers, but He is separate from them. He pervades the universe, yet He is above it and independent of it.

The Transcendence of God

God is exalted so far above the created universe that we cannot even imagine it. He is not only lofty and eminent; He stands apart from His creation in a different quality of being. He is "the blessed and only Sovereign, the King of kings and Lord of lords; who alone possesses immortality and dwells in unapproachable light; whom no man has seen *or can see*" (1 Tim. 6:15-16; compare John 1:18, "No man has seen God at any time").

He alone is entirely separate from the things of creation, including time and space. Man and the universe are not at all necessary to God's being or perfection. The Lord is enthroned on high and exalted above the heavens (Pss. 113:4-6; 108:5; 123:1) and "His sovereignty rules over all" (Ps. 103:19).

God is the source of the immense power of the universe. There is no law or power or fate which transcends Him since He alone is the absolute Sovereign.

There is a limitless gulf between God and every creature. He is as high above a man as He is above an amoeba, and as high above an archangel as He is above a man. Because of God's infinitude, finite differences like these are negligible to Him.

But if all this is so, how can we have any positive concepts about God at all? Can we hope to think the unthinkable and comprehend the incomprehensible? Or is God so transcendent that we can say nothing meaningful about Him?

The answer lies in intelligible divine self-revelation. God is transcendent, but this does not mean that He is in all respects unintelligible. Neither does this mean that He is unable to communicate with man. God has clearly revealed to man true things about His character and purposes.

As we saw in chapters 7 and 8, there is a sense in which everything, if pressed far enough, can become a mystery which goes beyond the understanding of mortal man. But even though we can't see far, we *can see something*.

This is especially true in the case of God's written self-disclosure to man, the Bible. There are many things in the Bible which transcend human understanding, and this book has been dealing with some of them. Nevertheless, in the Bible God clearly communicates His attributes, His love for man, His plan of redemption, and so forth. In it, He reveals that He is at once transcendent and immanent.

The Immanence of God

Even though God is beyond this space-time universe, He is also immanent within it. He did not simply create the universe and then withdraw to observe what would happen. Rather, the universe is a created entity which is totally dependent upon God for its continued existence.

God not only created the world; He also conserves and sustains it. He is the One who gives order and meaning to the cosmos (Col. 1:17; Heb. 1:3). The universe is not an illusion. Nor is it a product of time and chance. It is real. Its patterns can be detected and studied by man.

This concept of immanence, furthermore, is related to God's

omnipresence, because the whole of God is in every place (see chap. 9). But immanence takes us beyond the spatial idea. It focuses on God's intimacy with His creation and His personal relationship with creatures created in His image.

Christ's Sermon on the Mount emphasizes the immanence of our heavenly Father. God provides food for the birds of the air, and He beautifully arrays the lilies of the field (Matt. 6:26-30). He counts the number of the stars, makes the grass grow, and gives food to the beasts (Ps. 147:4-9; see Isa. 40:26). In the same way that God numbers the immense stars, He also numbers the hairs on every person's head (Matt. 10:30).

Paul's address to the Athenians spoke clearly about the immanence of God (Acts 17:24-28). He said that "in Him we live and move and exist" (v. 28). Immanence is also seen in God's intimate dealings with all men. "The steps of a man are established by the Lord; and He delights in his way. When he falls, he shall not be hurled headlong; because the Lord is the One who holds his hand" (Ps. 37:23-24).

The fact that "the ways of a man are before the eyes of the Lord, and He watches all his paths" (Prov. 5:21) can be comforting or disquieting depending on one's relation to the Lord. He knows the secrets of the heart and no one can do anything without God's complete knowledge (Ps. 44:21; see Isa. 29:15-16; Jer. 23:23-24). But those who are rightly related to God find peace and comfort in His presence. Nothing at all can separate Christians from God's love (Rom.8:38-39). "The eyes of the Lord are toward the righteous, and His ears are open to their cry. . . . The Lord is near to the brokenhearted, and saves those who are crushed in spirit" (Ps. 34:15, 18).

The incarnation of the Son of God is a special example of God's immanence. The great Creator entered into our little world in a unique way. He emptied Himself of His glory (Phil. 2:6-8) and submitted Himself to the conditions of humanity. Even before His incarnation, Christ was immanent, but not in the same way He was subsequent to it. Because of the incarnation, we can see what otherwise would have been hidden. "And the Word became flesh, and dwelt among us, and we beheld His glory. . . . No man has seen God at any time; the only begotten God, who is in the bosom of the Father, He has explained Him" (John 1:14, 18).

The indwelling of Christians by the Father, Son, and Holy Spirit is an example of God's specialized localization (see chap. 9). This indwelling of the Godhead is also a special example of the immanence of God. He is uniquely intimate with believers. However, even this is beyond our ability to imagine. What does indwelling mean? What mystery then is in the simple expression "you in Me, and I in you"! (John 14:20) "Where" is God inside a Christian?

Summary

God dwells in the universe, but He is nevertheless separated from it by an unbridgeable gap. God is immanent within His works but He is also transcendent above them. He is both near and far; intimate yet separate. "I dwell in a high and holy place, and also with the contrite and lowly of spirit" (Isa. 57:15).

Berkhof puts it this way: God is incomprehensible but yet knowable.[1] He is incomprehensible because of His transcendence but He is knowable because of His immanence. He is the infinite-personal God, the separate-indwelling God, the Creator-Redeemer, and the Author-Sustainer.

The transcendent-immanent God is the only adequate object of faith. Only the One who created all things (the transcendent God) has the power sufficient to redeem and recreate all things (the immanent God). The creative work and the redemptive work of God are thus bound together in the Scriptures.

Many biblical passages portray God as both transcendent and immanent. Some describe the personal appearances of God to different men. These include God's appearance to Moses in the burning bush on Mount Horeb (Ex. 3), His appearance to Job (Job 38:1—42:8), Isaiah's vision of God on His throne (Isa. 6), Ezekiel's vision of God's glory (Ezek. 1), and Saul's encounter with the resurrected Christ (Acts 9).

In every case these manifestations of God produced an overwhelming sense of terror and dismay because of the awesome power of the transcendent God. Each one of these men was painfully conscious of his own sinfulness when confronted with God's glory and holiness. Stott makes this comment about these encounters with the transcendent-immanent God:

> If the curtain which veils the unspeakable majesty of God could be drawn aside but for a moment, we too should not be able to bear the sight. As it is, we only dimly perceive

how pure and brilliant must be the glory of almighty God. However, we know enough to realize that sinful man while still in his sins can never approach this holy God. A great chasm yawns between God in His righteousness and man in his sin.[2]

One of the clearest examples of the biblical balance between these two truths is in Revelation 1:9-20. The Apostle John enjoyed a more intimate relationship with the Lord Jesus while He was on earth than any other man (see John 13:23; 19:26; 20:2; 21:7, 20). After Christ's ascension, this relationship continued because Christ indwelt John as He did other Christians. Nevertheless, when John saw Jesus in His glory, he "fell at His feet as a dead man" (Rev. 1:17). The Lord indwells believers (immanence), but He is also separate from them (transcendence).

The account in Exodus 33:18-23, where Moses talks with God and asks to see His glory, also shows these two aspects. No man can see the face of God and live (v. 20; transcendence), but Moses was allowed to see God's "back" (v. 23, immanence). So God allowed Moses to see His glory, but He had to protect him from it at the same time.

The Extremes

Two natural extremes relate to the transcendence-immanence antinomy. The transcendence extreme minimizes or denies God's immanence. Modern examples are found in Deism, some groups within Judaism, and Barth and Brunner, who tend to view God as "wholly Other." [3]

Deists emphasize human reason rather than revelation. The universe has no dependence on God. God is wholly transcendent and so out of reach that He might just as well not exist.

The immanence extreme minimizes or denies God's transcendence. The more popular current examples are Pantheism, Panentheism, Naturalism and Humanism, and the "Social Gospel."

Pantheism (monism) sees God as the process of history; He is the soul and reason of the universe. God is in us and we are all God.

Panentheism (Process Theology) is a liberal approach to natural theology which attacks the supernatural, transcendent idea of God.[4] Process theologians have abandoned the supernatural God.

Thus they are left with evolution instead of creation, "relationship" instead of redemption, and "analogy in human experience" instead of revelation.

Naturalists and humanists have an anti-transcendent outlook, allowing only the immanent. They hope that history somehow contains its own meaning. Given enough time, man will understand the world and all significant truth without having to turn to a reference point outside of himself. This is a man-centered faith in the human potential.

The "Social Gospel" strips all transcendent elements from Christianity and humanizes all religion including the conception of God. God is reduced to such a level that men should not submit to Him; they should just cooperate with Him. The only purpose of religion is to serve man, not God.[5]

We see from these brief examples that serious error is introduced when anyone minimizes or denies either of these biblical truths. The transcendence extreme leads to the idea of a God who is so "wholly Other" that He cannot be known or communicated with on a personal basis. The immanence extreme reduces God to our level and effectively destroys all hope for the redemption of sinful men and a fallen universe.

The only way to represent the biblical picture of reality is to acknowledge the revealed fact that God is *both* transcendent *and* immanent. The two truths must be kept in perfect balance. From God's higher perspective, they are friends, not enemies. And only the transcendent-immanent God can at once be the infinite Creator and the personal Redeemer.

Some Applications

One way to apply the biblical doctrine of transcendent-immanent God to daily living is to connect it with the idea of "the fear of the Lord." Because the almighty God is immanent, He genuinely affects every part of our lives. His greatness and His immanence require our utmost regard, respect, and esteem.

There is no person or thing which should be revered as much as God. Unfortunately, most people repress their thoughts about God, resist Him, or rationalize Him away. Instead of bowing to reality, they distort reality by fearing other things more than the living God. That is, they revere such things as success, financial security, and friendships much more than God. Many people, for example, fear the loss of worldly status more than they fear a wrong relationship with God.

The biblical concept of fear is that, like faith, it can be good or bad depending on the object in which it is placed. "The fear of man brings a snare, but he who trusts in the Lord will be exalted" (Prov. 29:25). The problem is that unless God is one's ultimate "fear-object," [6] the things man reveres and fears losing do not properly reflect reality.

This can happen with Christians who lean too much in the transcendence direction and forget the immanence of God. Even in Christian circles there is a temptation to put other things in a higher place of reverence than God (for instance, the desire to be accepted and esteemed by a group or organization).

When people forget or ignore God's immanence, God becomes so transcendent that He is no longer a fear-object. And this leads to sin: "When men no longer fear God, they transgress His laws without hesitation." [7] (See Ps. 36:1; Ecc. 8:11.)

Christians should maintain the concept of God as awesome and dreadful, remembering at the same time that He is also immanent. This does not mean that the believer in Christ should be afraid of God as a Person, for the real Christian knows that God loves him and gave His Son for him. But at the same time, we should never forget who God is.

While some Christians minimize God's immanence, others minimize His transcendence and tend to forget the awesomeness and holiness of God. When this happens, their attitudes and actions may reflect a self-assurance and disrespect for the Person of God. Some believers speak of God in a flippant manner, using glib phrases like "Trippin' out with Jesus" as though the high and exalted One (Isa. 57:15) were a drug.

Another area which requires a balanced view of the transcendent-immanent God is the nature of God's indwelling. Every Christian is indwelt by the triune God. But there is sometimes so much emphasis placed on the fact that Christ indwells believers that we fail to remember that Christ as the God-man is in heaven at the right hand of the Father.

Though Christ is in believers, the New Testament speaks much more about believers being "in Christ." A proper emphasis on what we are and have in Him (see the Book of Ephesians) will avoid an overbalance into internal mysticism. We should focus on the work that is going on in heaven at God's right hand on our behalf. This is where Christ is interceding for us (Rom. 8:34).

The transcendence-immanence antinomy relates to other antinomies and to different facets of the Christian life. It ties in closely with chapters 4, 5, and 9. In the problem of evil, for example (chap. 5), God in His holiness is outraged at sin (transcendence), but He continues to sustain the world and He personally suffers because of the sin (immanence). God does not watch the world with detached interest; He is involved.

In prayer and worship, believers can also sense both the otherness and the nearness of God. Though God is enthroned in His transcendence, He is at the same time very near in His graciousness and immanence.

When we see the Lord Jesus Christ face to face, what we now dimly perceive about the transcendent-immanent God will become so much more clear. Perhaps we will react as did two of the animals in *The Wind in the Willows* when they saw "the Piper at the Gates of Dawn":

> "Rat!" he found breath to whisper, shaking. "Are you afraid?"
>
> "Afraid?" murmured the Rat, his eyes shining with unutterable love. "Afraid! Of *Him?* O, never, never! And yet— and yet—O, Mole, I am afraid!"
>
> Then the two animals, crouching to the earth, bowed their heads and did worship.[8]

11 Positional Versus Experiential Truth

God views us in Christ as perfect. Nevertheless, the sin nature is still very much a part of us. The implications of these two contrary descriptions of saved people are so profound that they are unsearchable.

The Believer's Position in Christ
The mystery of the work of the cross is beyond comprehension. When someone appropriates the work of the cross by trusting in Christ, he is instantly placed in union with Christ. This union is so real that the believer has actually died and risen with Christ. The believer is included in the whole process of Christ's death, burial, resurrection, and present life in such a way that these things become completely identified with him. The Christian's life is now bound up with the life Christ lives before the Father.

God cannot lower His standards; He does not grade on a curve. God's standard of righteousness is complete perfection. Christ said, "Therefore you are to be perfect, as your heavenly Father is perfect" (Matt. 5:48). It has been said, "The righteousness which God requires is that righteousness which His righteousness requires Him to require." The substitutionary work of Jesus Christ was the only possible way in which God could justify (declare righteous) sinful men without compromising His own holiness (Rom. 3:26).

The Bible presents an astounding array of privileges that belong to a person the moment he becomes a child of God through faith in Jesus. Many of these blessings are discussed by Paul in the first three chapters of Ephesians. Others are to be found throughout the New Testament. Some of the better-known ones are mentioned below; a more complete list with Scripture has been compiled most ably by Lewis Sperry Chafer.[1]

Each of these positional truths, mind you, is the present possession of *every* believer.

Believers are all in God's eternal plan (see chap. 4). All Christians have been *redeemed* (purchased out of bondage to sin; Gal. 5:1; Eph. 1:7) and *reconciled* to God (2 Cor. 5:20-21). God has *forgiven* all the believer's trespasses (Eph. 1:7; Col. 2:13), and has *adopted* him into the family of God (Gal. 4:4-7; Eph. 1:4-5).

In the letter to the Romans, Paul concentrates on the fact that God has declared Christians righteous (*justified;* Rom. 3:24, 26; 4:5; 5:1). Peter writes that believers in Christ are "a chosen race, a royal priesthood, a holy nation, a people for God's own possession" (1 Peter 2:9).

Each person in Christ has direct access to God and His grace (Rom. 5:1-2; Eph. 2:18; Heb. 4:16). Believers are the objects of God's devotion, and He cares for us in many striking ways (Rom. 5:8-10).

God tells us that Christians are already as good as glorified (Rom. 8:30), for God sees believers as they will be: perfect and complete in Christ (Col. 2:9-10). We have already been given "every spiritual blessing . . . in Christ" (Eph. 1:3).

These positional blessings cannot be earned, since they are not related to human merit. Neither are they progressive in character, for they are all given to the believer at the moment of salvation. They do not depend on how we feel, for they are not emotionally experienced by the believer (for instance, Christians do not "feel" justification or sanctification).

The believer's position in Christ is eternal, because God gives these things to us as gifts which we do not deserve. They are based on God's grace, not human effort, and consequently, God will not revoke them. God alone makes these things possible, not man. If it were not for His revelation to man, we would not even know they were available to us as a free gift.

The Believer's Daily Experience

In spite of all these wonderful positional truths, it is still true that Christians are sinners. We have been cleansed from sin and made perfect in God's sight because of Christ's righteousness being placed to our account. But our daily experiences are imperfect.

From the believer's own perspective, he is painfully aware of his sinfulness (that is, if he is being honest enough with himself to admit it). None of us can attain a state of sinless perfection in this life. We cannot reach a plateau of complete purity as long as the sin nature is a part of us. John made this abundantly clear in the opening discussion of his first epistle (1 John 1:5—2:2).

"If we say that we have no sin, we are deceiving ourselves, and the truth is not in us" (1 John 1:8). John refers here to the fact that every believer still has the sin nature ("sin" is in distinction to "sins" or "sinned"). We would only be deceiving ourselves if we denied this truth.

John also refers to specific manifestations of the believer's sin nature: "If we say that we have not sinned, we make Him a liar" (v. 10). There is no question that believers commit sins. John says that it would compound the problem for a believer to act as though he did not sin on an occasion when he did sin. Instead, we should confess our sins for what they really are before the Lord, knowing that Christ is our Advocate with the Father (1:9; 2:1-2).

The old sin nature is still in the Christian even though he has also received a new nature or self, "which in the likeness of God has been created in righteousness and holiness of the truth" (Eph. 4:24). Now the Christian has a choice which he did not have before he received Christ. By the exercise of his will he can choose to walk in his new nature according to the Spirit, or he can walk in his old nature according to the flesh (Rom. 8:3-9).

However, no matter how passionately a believer may desire a quality of life which conforms perfectly to his position in the heavenlies, he cannot always maintain this standard. The most pious and godly men and women through the centuries have acknowledged their utter corruption before the holy God. As a person grows in Christ, he also becomes more conscious of his own sinfulness, and thus more appreciative of God's grace. The Apostle Paul described his life as a constant struggle of the old against the new (Rom. 7:14—8:2). He wrote "For that which I am doing, I do not understand; for I am not practicing what I would like to do, but I am doing the very thing I hate. . . . For the good that I wish, I do not do; but I practice the very evil that I do not wish" (vv. 15, 19). Paul undoubtedly found a much more victorious life than this (see 7:24-25), but he was also able to distinguish the reality of a defeated Christian life from his position in the heavenlies in Christ Jesus. This is why he could victoriously proclaim, "There is therefore now no condemnation for those who are in Christ Jesus" (8:1).

Clearly, there is a great difference between our subjective experience of salvation and our objective salvation which is secure at the right hand of the Father. There is a difference between the believer's state (experiential truth) and his standing (positional truth). The believer's state is changeable but his standing is unchangeable.[2] The real difficulty lies in how both things can be true of a person at once.

How to Avoid the Extremes

The two natures (old and new) are contrary to one another (Gal. 5:17), but believers in Christ have both. Because of the reality of both positional and experiential truth, the believer is at once a saint and a sinner. God will not indwell an unclean vessel, but He indwells every Christian. Even though He knows that we are still sinners, He also sees the righteousness of Christ Jesus which has been placed to our account. In addition, He sees us as we will be, when our sin nature will be removed (this relates to the time antinomy, chap. 7).

Two basic extremes can arise if Christians do not properly approach positional and experiential truth. The first extreme results from minimizing positional truth. This produces a mentality of fear and insecurity. Unaware of his position in Christ, the believer does not understand that God fully recognizes how bad he is and yet accepts him through the merits of Christ.

Such a person is still operating on a performance basis, hoping to please God, but constantly afraid of being exposed. He falsely equates his experience with the status of his salvation, and he is therefore still under the curse of "religiosity." He may feel that unless he confesses all his sins he will not be positionally forgiven and in danger of losing his salvation.

Even if salvation were based 99% on the work of Christ and 1% on human effort, there could be no genuine security and peace with God. Everyone would be worrying about that 1%. The only foundation on which a real love relationship with God can be built is the biblical revelation that Christ has paid for all the believer's sins.

Only God Himself could satisfy His demand for complete righteousness. This is why it is so important for believers to *reckon by faith* that the positional things God says about them are really so.

The second extreme results from minimizing our experiential walk. Some Christians feel that since they are rightly related to God positionally, they can be careless about being right experientially.

The Bible says, *"If we confess our sins, He is faithful and righteous to forgive us our sins and to cleanse us from all unrighteousness"* (1 John 1:9). Some shrug that *if* phrase off with, "My sins have already been forgiven!" But John is not denying that Christ has positionally forgiven the believer's sins. Rather, he is writing about the believer's fellowship with a holy God. While sin and disobedience cannot annul a Christian's position, they can and will seriously mar his walk with God.

It is important to notice that the believer's position versus his experience ties in closely with the divine sovereignty/human responsibility antinomy (chap. 4). Divine sovereignty connects with the believer's position, and human responsibility relates to his experience. Therefore, the same balance that is required in our approach to divine sovereignty and human responsibility is also essential to a proper understanding of positional and experiential truth.

Even though a Christian's position is secure with God, he should not adopt the attitude that he can do as he pleases. He is still responsible to live a life of quality that reflects his heavenly position to the world. In one way he should be sure to distinguish position and experience, especially in the area of salvation. But in another way, position and experience should be joined together.

The believer's position ought to be the basis for his experience. This is clearly seen in an epistle like Ephesians. After Paul outlines the believer's position in the heavenlies (Eph. 1—3), he then builds a whole series of imperatives (Eph. 4—6) on this foundation. There are no commands in the positional section of the book because these are things which have been accomplished by God alone. But then the imperatives begin to appear, always based on positional truth.

When Experience Will Equal Position

There is a constant struggle in Christians between the old and the new natures, and *nothing* can eliminate it until the old sin nature is removed. Only then will the believer's experience perfectly conform to his position. Until that time, he must trust God to help him make his experience move closer to his position.

When will perfection come? Paul says that we are groaning within ourselves, eagerly waiting for the redemption of our body (Rom. 8:23). He also says that believers must all appear before the judgment seat of Christ (2 Cor. 5:10), and that each man's work will become evident in that day (1 Cor. 3:11-15). This is a resurrection of life (John 5:25-29) and a judgment of rewards, not condemnation. Even if all of a believer's work is burned up, "he shall suffer loss; but he himself shall be saved, yet so as through fire" (1 Cor. 3:15).

At the judgment seat of Christ the old nature will be stripped from us. It is possible that for the first time we will see our sins as Christ sees them, as our dead works are being burned up. From that point on, our experience will be identical with our position because the capacity to sin will be gone.

Now believers are positionally righteous because they have received Christ. But our hope is set on the time when we see Christ and become altogether righteous by nature.

Applications

Believers must clearly focus on two things: the divine side of salvation (position) and human responsibility (experience). When positional truth is properly understood, it can become a great aid to our daily experience. This is why Paul said that we are consciously to consider our position in Christ to be true of us, regardless of how we feel.

> Even so consider yourselves to be dead to sin, but alive to God in Christ Jesus.
> Therefore do not let sin reign in your mortal body that you should obey its lusts, and do not go on presenting the members of your body to sin as instruments of unrighteous-

ness; but present yourselves to God as those alive from the dead, and your members as instruments of righteousness to God (Rom. 6:11-13).

Not only are we to reckon our position as true in our lives; we must also *act* (human responsibility) on the basis of this truth. Even though the believer possesses every spiritual blessing (Eph. 1:3), these will do nothing for his everyday life unless he starts to make use of them. Too many Christians live like spiritual paupers because they ignore the limitless riches that God makes available to them.

12 The Word of God

"I believe that God has revealed Himself to men, and that revelation is the Bible." Thus we began (p. 11) and there we stand: the Bible is *the* authority for truth. However, even God's revealed Word involves a mysterious element which is beyond human comprehension. Like the God-man, the Bible is completely divine and completely human at once.

The Bible Is a Product of God

Revelation has been defined as God's communicating to man the things that man otherwise would not know. If this is carried back far enough, it includes all knowledge. This is why revelation is often divided into two basic kinds: (1) natural or general revelation, and (2) supernatural or special revelation. According to Scripture, the creation itself reveals things about God, including His existence, His divine nature, and His eternal power (Ps. 19:1-4; Rom. 1:18-20). This revelation is sufficient to condemn those who reject God (Rom. 1:20, "they are without excuse").

But God reveals much more about Himself through special revelation. He is the One who took the initiative in revelation, and He did it through a variety of means.

He revealed Himself by special actions and appearances to men (the pillar of fire and the Angel of the Lord). Many times He spoke to men in dreams and visions. Sometimes He used special means of revelation like the Urim and Thummim on the breastplate of the high priest or the casting of the lot. More often, however, he communicated directly to men as He did with Moses, the prophets, and the apostles.

The *climax* of revelation, called personal revelation, was realized in the incarnation of Jesus Christ, the God-man (see John 1:18; 14:9; Col. 1:15; Heb. 1:1-3).

One type of special revelation is written revelation. The Bible is not only a record of revelation; it is also a revelation itself. This is so because the very act of writing Scripture was personally superintended by God the Holy Spirit. This is part of the biblical doctrine of *inspiration*.

Ryrie defines inspiration as "God's superintendence of the human authors so that, using their own individual personalities, they composed and recorded without error His revelation to man in the words of the original autographs." [1] There is no way to understand how God worked with the human authors in such a way that the resultant Scriptures were at once *their own writings* and *God's infallible Word*. This is the antinomy.

The Bible clearly claims to be a product of God. "All Scripture is inspired by God and profitable for teaching, for reproof, for correction, for training in righteousness" (2 Tim. 3:16). The word *inspired* in this verse is a word coined by Paul which literally means "God-breathed." Scripture is the breath of God.

A second classic passage is: "No prophecy was ever made by an act of human will, but men moved by the Holy Spirit spoke from God" (2 Peter 1:21). Combining these verses, "inspiration is the process by which Spirit-moved writers recorded God-breathed writings." [2]

Inspiration applies to *all* parts of all canonical (inspired) books. Because the inspired Scriptures partake of the nature of God, they are without error. Everything the Bible teaches is true, including its historical and factual statements. The very words themselves were inspired in the original manuscripts (see Jer. 26:2; Matt. 5:18; 21:42; Luke 16:17; 24:44; John 10:35; Rom. 3:2; 15:4; 1 Cor. 2:13; Heb. 10:7; 2 Pet. 3:16; Rev. 22:18-19). Christ and Paul built whole arguments on specific words used in the Old Testament (see Matt. 22:41-45; John 10:34-35; Gal. 3:16).

It is clear that the doctrine of inspiration applies to the autographs (the original manuscripts), not to the translations and later manuscripts. Nevertheless, the science of textual criticism (or "lower criticism") demonstrates the accuracy of our Hebrew and Greek manuscripts. Only small details are in question, and none of these affect any biblical doctrine. Our Bibles are substantially pure, and they can be received with confidence as virtually inspired.[3]

Men have held and taught inadequate and unbiblical theories of inspiration throughout church history. One theory proposes that inspiration is a natural (though God-given) genius for expression. The Bible is inspired in the same way that great art is inspired.

Another theory confuses inspiration with *illumination*. It sees men of God being given special understanding of God's will and recording their insights in the books which came to be included in the Bible. This, however, is not inspiration but illumination, a ministry of the Holy Spirit which provides us with spiritual understanding of the truths of Scripture.

The neoorthodox view states that the Bible *becomes* the Word of God only in an existential experience or a crisis encounter with God.

The endorsement theory holds that God simply gave His stamp of approval to the spiritual writings of godly men. These writings become His Word because He uses them in blessing men.

The concept theory teaches that God gave the human authors His inspired ideas or concepts. These authors then expressed the concepts in their own words.

Another theory teaches that the Bible contains different degrees of inspiration. That is, the control by the Holy Spirit in inspiration fluctuates with the receptivity of the human authors and/or the character of the material. A variation of this theory is the idea that only parts of the Bible are inspired: namely, those portions of Scripture which could not have been written by unaided men.

The (mechanical) dictation theory regards the human writers as secretaries who simply recorded the dictation of God. Liberal theologians sometimes build this idea into a straw man which they claim represents the conservative position. When they knock it over, they assume that they have refuted the "fundamentalists." But in reality, very few evangelical theologians hold this view. They recognize that the human writers were involved as authors of the Scripture.

It is clear that the Bible repeatedly claims to be a direct product of God. It is fully inspired in all its words and parts (verbal, plenary inspiration). It is God's propositional revelation to all people, breathed by the Spirit of God. The stamp of "thus says the Lord" pervades the pages of Scripture. This is why the Bible accomplishes such phenomenal results in lives (see Isa. 55:11).

The Bible is unlike any other book; its Author constantly goes with it and empowers it according to His purpose. It is a living book because it is animated by the Holy Spirit. "For the Word of God is living and active and sharper than any two-edged sword, and piercing as far as the division of soul and spirit, of both joints and marrow, and able to judge the thoughts and intentions of the heart" (Heb. 4:12).

The Bible Is a Product of Men

Not only is the Bible completely divine; it is also completely human. This is not difficult to demonstrate since the human authors of so many of the books are clearly identified. The authors of most of the psalms name themselves (David, Asaph, and others). Solomon says he wrote most of the Proverbs, and the prophets identify their works as well. The authors of most of the New Testament books record their names in the opening sentences.

The humanity of the biblical books is also supported by the obvious personality and literary differences. The writers had differing styles, vocabularies, grammar, and backgrounds. These differences are seen in translations, and they are even more evident in the original languages. In addition to this, the Scriptures also express personal human desires and thoughts. For example, Paul wrote: "When you come bring the cloak which I left at Troas with Carpus, and the books, especially the parchments" (2 Tim. 4:13). This does not sound like a passage simply dictated to Paul by God. It was Paul who needed his cloak, not God!

The Uniqueness of Biblical Revelation

The biblical doctrine of revelation is quite unique, since it alone claims to be equally a product of God and man. The Bible is a completely divine and completely human book in a way that we cannot comprehend. Other so-called scriptures either claim to be the insights of spiritual sages (the Hindu scriptures), or dictated messages from God (the *Koran* and the *Book of Mormon*). Only the Bible is a God-man revelation. It has infinite depth of content but it is couched in finite human language.

This antinomy parallels the divine sovereignty/human responsibility antinomy (chap. 4). The Bible is God's revelation to man, and His sovereignty ensured that it is completely authoritative and inspired. But this does not mean that God restricted the free will of the various human authors. Instead, they were able to exercise their free wills and human responsibilities even while writing the words that were at once human and divine.

The Two Extremes

People do not *naturally* arrive at the proper view of Scripture. An antinomy exists here and gives rise to two natural extremes. One minimizes the divine aspect of the Bible by humanizing it. The opposite extreme minimizes the human aspect of the Bible by deifying it.

The first of these extremes states that since the Bible was written by men, it cannot also be the pure revelation of God. It contains great truths, but being human in origin, it is not free from error.

The popularity of this view is seen in the prevalence of the inadequate theories of inspiration (mentioned earlier in this chapter). All but the last of these play down (in varying degrees) the divine aspect of the Scriptures. Thus, these theories adequately explain the human aspect of the Bible (personality, stylistic, vocabulary, and grammatical differences), but at the great cost of weakening or completely eliminating the divine. They fail to honor the Bible's own claims to be more than just the writings of men.

The second extreme is represented by the (mechanical) dictation theory. This view does not account for the human aspect of the Bible which is seen in the personality and literary differences. It can also lead to bibliolatry (the worship of the Bible instead of the God who revealed it).

The Analogy to the God-man

There is a close parallel between Christ as the living Word and the Scriptures as the written Word of God. Both the Saviour and the Scriptures have divine-human natures. In both cases the process by which this product came about is beyond human comprehension.

In the case of the God-man, God joined with sinful humanity to produce "the holy offspring" (Luke 1:35). This verse teaches that the Holy Spirit came upon Mary, and the power of the Most High overshadowed her. In the case of the written Word, God again joined with sinful humanity to produce His holy Word. The Holy Spirit moved men to speak from God (2 Pet. 1:21). Because of this, the living Word is sinless and the written Word is without error (in the original manuscripts).[4]

On the negative side, the analogy between the two Words can be seen in the way that both can and have been abused by the same two extremes. One minimizes the Word's divinity and the other extreme minimizes the humanity. The only proper approach is to trust God and bow to His greater wisdom by acknowledging the complete divinity and humanity of Christ and the Scriptures.

Some Applications

Just as the Bible is the result of a divine-human process, it requires a divine-human process for people to appreciate it and understand it properly today. The difference is that the "encoding" of the Word was infallible, but the "decoding" of it is fallible.

In order to understand the truths of God's Word, Christians must place themselves under the guidance of the Holy Spirit. Apart from this illuminating ministry of the Holy Spirit, there can be no spiritual receptiveness to the truths of God. This is the divine aspect of the process. Tozer comments, "There is no truth apart from the Spirit. The most brilliant intellect may be imbecilic when confronted with the mysteries of God. For a man to understand revealed truth requires an act of God equal to the original act which inspired the text." [5]

The human aspect of the decoding process is also critical. Illumination must be accompanied by logical consistency on our part. Certain basic interpretive principles must be followed in attempting to understand the Bible. This is the science of hermeneutics.

We should approach the Scriptures in a plain and normal fashion. Each passage should be examined in the light of the immediate and broad context. In this way, if a symbol or parable or figure of speech is being used, the context will generally make this clear.

The Bible should be understood in a historical and grammatical way, and this in-context approach must be applied consistently to all parts of the Scriptures. Furthermore, Scripture is its own best interpreter. We should always allow the clear passages to interpret the unclear.

When these principles of hermeneutics are not consistently followed, difficulties arise. Thus, various cults make the Bible say what they want it to say by simply pulling passages out of context.

Every time we read the Bible, we should remember that our understanding of it must be a divine-human process. This is why it is wise to pray for the guidance and illumination of the Holy Spirit before we study a portion of Scripture.

Witnessing is another divine-human process. The Spirit of God works through the Word of God in the hands of the children of God to bring people to Christ. God has chosen to work through people to lead other people to the Saviour. Witnessing is most effective when the Word of God is unleashed in the hands of believers.

Finally, believers need to develop a greater appreciation for the Word. God has given us an infinite revelation that has the answers for which people are searching. We should praise God for His written revelation. It is a message that gives us wisdom, instruction, correction, and encouragement (Rom. 15:4; 2 Tim. 3:16). But it is also a propositional revelation that always demands a response on the part of the reader.

Epilogue

We have frequently observed that certain antinomies relate to other antinomies. Now we can go one step further: *every* antinomy relates to every other antinomy. This is because God is the Author of reality. In an *ultimate* sense, everything can be traced back to the Person and plan of God. All the incomprehensibles revealed in Scripture connect together because they are the product of God's higher wisdom (see fig. 4).

By this time it should be clear that we who are finite cannot comprehend everything about the infinite God. But we *can* comprehend enough about God through His revelation to speak meaningful things about Him. The Good News of salvation, for instance, has been so clearly communicated that even children can appropriate this message by receiving Christ as their personal Saviour from sin.

What, then, is my God? What, I ask, except the Lord *God? For who is Lord but the Lord? Or who is God save our God?* O highest and best, most powerful, most all-powerful, most merciful and most just, most deeply hidden and most nearly present, most beautiful and most strong, constant yet incomprehensible, changeless, yet changing all things, never new, never old, making all things new; *bringing the proud to decay and they know it not;* always acting and always at rest; still gathering yet never wanting; upholding, filling and protecting, creating, nourishing, and bringing to perfection; seeking, although in need of nothing. You love, but with no storm of passion; You are jealous, but with no anxious fear; You repent, but do not grieve; in Your anger calm; You change Your works, but never change Your plan; You take back what You find and yet have never lost; never in need, You are yet glad of gain; never greedy, yet still demanding profit on Your loans; to be paid in excess, so that You may be the debtor, and yet who has anything which is not Yours? You pay back debts which You never owed and cancel debts without losing anything. And in all this what have I said, my God, my Life, my holy sweetness? What does any man succeed in saying when he attempts to speak of You? Yet woe to those who do not speak of You at all, when those who speak most say nothing.

—*The Confessions of St. Augustine,* 1. 4.

"Great is our Lord, and abundant in strength; His understanding is infinite" (Ps. 147:5).

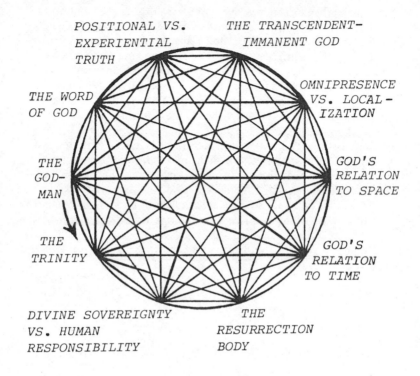

POSITIONAL VS.
EXPERIENTIAL
TRUTH

THE TRANSCENDENT-
IMMANENT GOD

THE WORD
OF GOD

OMNIPRESENCE
VS. LOCAL-
IZATION

THE
GOD-
MAN

GOD'S
RELATION
TO SPACE

THE
TRINITY

GOD'S
RELATION
TO TIME

DIVINE SOVEREIGNTY
VS. HUMAN
RESPONSIBILITY

THE
RESURRECTION
BODY

FIGURE 4

Begin with the God-man antinomy and consider how it relates to each one of the others. Then go to the Trinity antinomy and do the same, and so on in a counterclockwise direction, until you finally come back to the God-man antinomy.

Notes

CHAPTER 2

1. This problem of the eternal generation of the Son from the Father represents a unique situation, if not another antinomy. Some passages which show that Christ was the Son of God prior to His incarnation are: Psalm 2:7, Isaiah 9:6, John 3:16-17, and Galatians 4:4. The nature of this sonship and of this "generation" are clearly unique, and they relate to the antinomy of time (see chap. 7).

2. S. U. Zuidema, *Kierkegaard* (Philadelphia: Presbyterian and Reformed Publishing Company, 1960).

CHAPTER 3

1. David H. Freeman, *Tillich* (Philadelphia: Presbyterian and Reformed Publishing Company, 1962), pp. 10 ff.

2. John F. Walvoord, in *Jesus Christ Our Lord* (Chicago: Moody Press, 1969), pp. 51-54, shows that the Angel of the Lord, who appears many times in the Old Testament, is a theophany of the preincarnate Christ.

3. B. B. Warfield, "Trinity," *The International Standard Bible Encyclopaedia*, ed. by James Orr (5 vols.; Grand Rapids: Wm. B. Eerdmans Publishing Co., 1939), V, 3012.

4. R. A. Finlayson, "Trinity," *The New Bible Dictionary*, ed. by J. D. Douglas (Grand Rapids: Wm. B. Eerdmans Publishing Co., 1962), 1300.

5. Sometimes the term *ontological Trinity* is used of the triune God to refer to His activity within Himself in His essential nature. This is distinguished from the term *economic Trinity* which describes His activity with respect to His created universe. Here the Father is especially active as the Originator, Creator, and Sustainer. The Son is the Revealer and Redeemer. The Holy Spirit is active in executing the creative-redemptive plan of God.

6. "The diversity and the unity in the Godhead are . . . equally ultimate; they are exhaustively correlative to one another and not correlative to any-

thing else" (Cornelius Van Til, "Apologetics" [unpublished class syllabus, Westminster Theological Seminary, n.d.], p. 8). Also compare Carnell's statement: "The essence of Deity—the One—is equally exhausted in the Persons—the Many" (Edward John Carnell, *An Introduction to Christian Apologetics* [Grand Rapids: Wm. B. Eerdmans Publishing Co., 1948], p. 41, n. 22).

7. Henry M. Morris, *The Bible and Modern Science* (Chicago: Moody Press, 1951), pp. 24-25.

8. Henry M. Morris, *Biblical Cosmology and Modern Science* (Nutley, N.J.: Craig Press, 1970), p. 40.

9. Walter Martin, *The Kingdom of the Cults* (Minneapolis: Bethany Fellowship, 1965), p. 47.

10. *Ibid.*, p. 178. Mormonism is actually polytheistic since it indicates that there are other gods besides these three.

11. Hinduism is a pantheistic religion since it teaches that everything including good and evil is God. This particular group of three gods is really symbolic of the being, becoming, and dissolution of the universe, a process which continues on and on in unlimited cycles.

12. Finlayson, "Trinity," p. 1300.

CHAPTER 4

1. Lewis Carroll, *The Annotated Alice* (New York: Clarkson N. Potter, 1960), p. 251.

2. Here are some other passages which support divine election and sovereignty: Exodus 14:17; Deuteronomy 29:4; 32:39; 1 Samuel 2:25; 9:15—10:9; 2 Samuel 12:11; 1 Kings 22:23; 1 Chronicles 10:14; Job 14:5; 38:1—42:3; Psalms 33:10-11; 47:7-8; 75:6-8; 102:18; 104:1-35; 139:16; Isaiah 14:24; 40:12-26; 53:10; 55:11; Jeremiah 10:23; 15:2; Daniel 2:21; 4:17; Amos 4:7; Matthew 10:29-30; Luke 10:21; Acts 13:48; Romans 8:29-30; Ephesians 3:11; 2 Timothy 1:9; Revelation 17:17.

3. J. l. Packer, *Evangelism and the Sovereignty of God* (Chicago: Inter-Varsity Press, 1967), p. 22. Compare James 4:12.

4. *Ibid.*, p. 23 (italics his).

5. Also compare Matthew 24:31; 25:34; John 6:44, 65; Acts 13:48 ("and as many as had been appointed to eternal life believed"); 16:14; Ephesians 1:4-5, 11; 2 Thessalonians 2:13; 1 Peter 1:1-2; Revelation 17:8.

6. John R. W. Stott, *Basic Christianity* (Downers Grove, Ill.: Inter-Varsity Press, 1958), p. 94.

7. Some other passages which emphasize the human responsibility to respond to the offer of salvation include Acts 13:38-39; Romans 1:16; 3:22, 26, 28; 4:5; 10:9-10; Galatians 3:22; Revelation 3:20.

8. John Warwick Montgomery, *Where is History Going?* (Minneapolis: Bethany Fellowship, 1969), p. 160.

9. Kenneth G. Howkins, *The Challenge of Religious Studies* (Downers Grove, Illinois: Inter-Varsity Press, 1972), p. 24.

10. Jay E. Adams, *Competent to Counsel* (Philadelphia: Presbyterian and Reformed Publishing Company, 1970), p. 6.

CHAPTER 5

1. This term comes from Hugh Silvester's book, *Arguing With God* (Downers Grove, Illinois: InterVarsity Press, 1971). This book, along with Edward J. Carnell's *An Introduction to Christian Apologetics* (Grand Rapids: Wm. B. Eerdmans Publishing Co., 1948), is helpful in dealing with the problem of evil. Also see John W. Wenham, *The Goodness of God* (Downers Grove, Illinois: InterVarsity Press, 1974).

2. Compare Gleason L. Archer, Jr., *A Survey of Old Testament Introduction* (Chicago: Moody Press, 1964), p. 182, n. 10.

3. Silvester, *Arguing,* p. 36.

4. Carnell, *Apologetics,* p. 277.

5. *Ibid.,* p. 302.

6. Robert D. Culver, "The Nature and Origin of Evil," *Bibliotheca Sacra,* CXXIX (April-June 1972), 108.

7. Clark H. Pinnock, "The Moral Argument for Christian Theism," *Bibliotheca Sacra,* CXXXI (April-June 1974), 117.

8. C. S. Lewis, "De Futilitate" in *Christian Reflections,* ed. by Walter Hooper (Grand Rapids: Wm. B. Eerdmans Publishing Co., 1967), pp. 69-70.

9. Francis Schaeffer, *Pollution and the Death of Man* (Wheaton, Illinois: Tyndale House Publishers, 1970), pp. 31-32.

10. Carnell, *Apologetics,* p. 295. (Italics his.)

11. Erwin W. Lutzer, *The Morality Gap* (Chicago: Moody Press, 1972), p. 102 (n).

12. C. S. Lewis, *The Problem of Pain* (New York: The Macmillan Company, 1962), pp. 127-28. (Italics his.)

CHAPTER 6

1. The Septuagint translates Psalm 16:9-11 in a way that speaks more directly of the hope of the resurrection from the dead, and Peter quotes this version of the psalm as a prophecy of Christ's resurrection in Acts 2:25-32.

2. The Bible says little about the resurrection bodies of unbelievers. We know that they will be resurrected (Dan. 12:2; John 5:28-29; Acts 24:15), but their bodies evidently will not be glorified (Dan. 12:2). The characteristics of Christ's risen body cannot be applied to theirs, and neither can the descriptions of 1 Corinthians 15. They will be cast into the lake of fire (Rev. 20:11-15) in their resurrected bodies.

3. J. A. Schep, *The Nature of the Resurrection Body* (Grand Rapids, Michigan: Wm. B. Eerdmans Publishing Co., 1964), p. 136.

4. *Ibid.*, p. 203.

5. Michael Green, *Man Alive* (Downers Grove, Illinois: InterVarsity Press, 1972), p. 82.

6. Alfred Edersheim, *The Life and Times of Jesus the Messiah* (London: Longmans, Green, and Co., 1886), II, 398-99.

CHAPTER 7

1. The only way a neutrino can be stopped is by a direct collision with other elementary particles. Such collisions are extremely unlikely, but they do occur because of the terrific number of neutrinos that pass through the earth at all times.

2. Edward F. Hills, *Space Age Science* (Des Moines, Iowa: The Christian Research Press, 1964), p. 122.

3. Lincoln Barnett, *The Universe and Dr. Einstein* (2nd rev. ed.; New York: Harper & Row, 1948), pp. 46-47. In a way, Aristotle anticipated this idea when he suggested that if other heavens exist they must have their own time, meaning that there would be many times at the same time.

4. James Reid, *God, the Atom, and the Universe* (Grand Rapids: Zondervan Publishing House, 1968), pp. 61-63.

5. *Ibid.*, p. 64.

6. George Gamow, *One, Two, Three . . . Infinity* (New York: The Viking Press, Inc., 1947), p. 105.

7. Another nasty theoretical effect of exceeding the speed of light is that time would be converted into space and space into time (Hills, *Space Age Science,* p. 32).

8. For instance, "At the speed of light one would weigh more than the universe, but be too small to measure, and would live forever, in no time!" (Reid, *God, the Atom, and the Universe,* p. 70)

9. John Warwick Montgomery, *Principalities and Powers* (Minneapolis: Bethany Fellowship, 1973), p. 125.

10. J. B. Priestly, *Man and Time* (New York: Crescent Books, 1964), p. 292.

11. Charles Caldwell Ryrie, *A Survey of Bible Doctrine* (Chicago: Moody Press, 1972), p. 23.

12. John C. Whitcomb, Jr. adds that in God's creative work "it is impossible to imagine a time interval in the transition from nonexistence to existence! . . . At one moment there was no light; the next moment there was!" (*The Early Earth* [Grand Rapids: Baker Book House, 1972], p. 25). One interesting thing along this line comes from Genesis 1:14-19. If the passage is taken in its plain and normal sense (that is, "day" equals a 24-hour period; see Ex. 20:11), it means that God created not only the stars but also the *light* from the stars to the earth. So light from a star one billion light years away is not necessarily one billion years old. It would only be as old as the interval from the fourth day of creation until now, even though it has an appearance of greater age.

13. A. W. Tozer, *The Divine Conquest* (Harrisburg: Christian Publications, 1950), p. 21.

14. Martin Gardner, "Can Time Go Backward?" *Scientific American,* January 1967, p. 108.

15. C. S. Lewis, "On 'Special Providences,' " Appendix B of *Miracles,* in *The Best of C. S. Lewis* (New York: The Iversen Associates, 1969), p. 375. Incidentally, Lewis makes an interesting observation on the subject of time and prayer on the next page: "Most of our prayers if fully analysed, ask either for a miracle or for events whose foundation will have to have been laid before I was born, indeed, laid when the universe began" (*Ibid.,* p. 376). Lewis goes on to conclude that a prayer at noon could become a contributing cause of an event which occurred two hours earlier (*Ibid.,* pp. 377-379).

16. F. Duane Lindsey, "Essays Toward a Theology of Beauty, Part I: God Is Beautiful," *Bibliotheca Sacra,* CXXXI (April—June 1974), 134.

17. C. S. Lewis, "Historicism," in *Christian Reflections,* ed. by Walter

Hooper (Grand Rapids: William B. Eerdmans Publishing Co., 1967), p. 113.

18. Joseph Campbell, "On Mystic Shapes of Things to Come—Circular and Linear," *Horizon*, 1974, p. 35. Priestly, *Man and Time*, p. 172. Geoffrey Parrinder, *A Dictionary of Non-Christian Religions* (Philadelphia: The Westminster Press, 1971).

19. J. R. R. Tolkein, *The Fellowship of the Ring* (2nd. ed.; Boston: Houghton Mifflin Company, 1965), p. 243. See John W. Montgomery, *et. al.*, *Myth, Allegory, and Gospel* (Minneapolis: Bethany Fellowship, 1974), pp. 127-129.

20. C. S. Lewis, *The Lion, the Witch and the Wardrobe* (New York: The Macmillan Company, 1950). Just the opposite effect can be found in Lord Dunsany's *The King of Elfland's Daughter* (New York: Ballantine Books, 1969), p. 28. In this fantasy, Alveric, a prince from our world, goes into a twilight world named Elfland for less than a day. When he returns everyone is 10 to 12 years older.

21. Oscar Cullmann, *Christ and Time* (rev. ed.; Philadelphia: The Westminster Press, 1964), p. 46.

22. *Ibid.*, p. 63.

23. J. A. Schep, *The Nature of the Resurrection Body* (Grand Rapids: William B. Eerdmans Publishing Co., 1964), p. 216.

24. A. W. Tozer, *The Knowledge of the Holy* (New York: Harper & Row, 1961), pp. 52-53.

CHAPTER 8

1. Arthur Koestler, *The Roots of Coincidence* (New York: Random House, 1972), pp. 50-53.

2. Lincoln Barnett, *The Universe and Dr. Einstein* (2nd. rev. ed.; New York: Harper & Row, 1948), p. 29.

3. Koestler, *The Roots*, p. 57.

4. George Gamow, *One, Two, Three . . . Infinity* (New York: The Viking Press, Inc., 1947), p. 100. The three changes which are brought about by relativistic speeds are (1) dilation of time, (2) contraction of space, and (3) increase in mass.

5. Barnett, *The Universe*, p. 85.

6. "Calculations show that an object as dense as a neutron star must also have prodigiously concentrated gravity—a hundred billion times that of earth. So strong is the gravitational pull that a neutron-star mountain could rise no more than an inch, and to climb it would take more energy than your metabolism can create in a lifetime" (Kenneth F. Weaver, "The Incredible Universe," *National Geographic*, May 1974, p. 618).

7. Each complete cycle would take, according to some estimates, about 80 billion years. But even with this "pulsating universe" idea, the process could not last forever. Each successive bang would have less available energy unless new energy were being formed out of nothing.

8. See Barnett, *The Universe*, p. 106, and Oscar L. Brauer, "God of the Universe Watching Over the Earth," *Creation Research Society Quarterly*, January 1967, p. 7.

9. See Gamow, *Infinity*, pp. 297-298, and Max Born, *Einstein's Theory of Relativity* (New York: Dover Publications, Inc., 1962), p. 345.

10. The biblical support of this important fact is impressive. Other references which clearly teach that God is the Creator of all that exists are: Genesis 2:1; Exodus 20:11; 31:17; 2 Kings 19:15; 1 Chronicles 16:26; 2 Chronicles 2:12; Nehemiah 9:6; Job 9:8-9; 26:7; 38:4-7, Psalms 8:3; 19:1; 89:11; 90:2; 95:5; 102:25; 104; 121:2; 124:8; 134:3; 136:5-7; 146:6; 148:5; Proverbs 16:4; Isaiah 40:26, 28; 45:18; Jeremiah 27:5; 32:17; 33:2; 51:15; Amos 4:13; 9:6; Jonah 1:9; Zechariah 12:1; Mark 13:19; John 1:3, 10; Acts 14:15; 17:24; Romans 1:19-20, 1 Corinthians 8:6; Ephesians 3:9; Colossians 1:16; Hebrews 1:2, 10; 2:10; 2 Peter 3:5; Revelation 4:11; 10:6; 14:7.

11. James F. Coppedge, *Evolution: Possible or Impossible?* (Grand Rapids: Zondervan Publishing House, 1973), pp. 208-211, includes a number of speculations about the location of heaven and hell. Here are four of the guesses he makes: (1) Hell may relate to the places of zero volume caused by gravitational collapse predicted by Penrose's theorem. (2) Two things could occupy the same space (he cites the empty space in atoms). We may not be able to detect the other realm even though it is coincident with our own. (3) Hell may be inside some black hole. (4) Heaven and hell may be too distant for detection (Coppedge therefore considers the possibility of instant space travel). However, the addition of another spatial dimension rather than placing heaven and hell in three-dimensional space seems to be a more satisfactory concept (see 1 Kings 8:27; 2 Cor. 12:2). Reid (*God, the Atom, and the Universe*, p. 81) makes this observation: "One more dimension would provide mankind with an unlimited heaven(s) which might be reached by simply stepping out or up, into the next dimension."

12. A. W. Tozer, *The Knowledge of the Holy* (New York: Harper & Row, 1961), pp. 33-34.

CHAPTER 9

1. Lewis Sperry Chafer, *Systematic Theology* (8 vols.; Dallas: Dallas Seminary Press, 1947), I, 221.

2. *The Confessions of St. Augustine, trans.* by Rex Warner (New York: The New American Library, 1963), pp. 18-19.

3. See John Warwick Montgomery's critique of pantheism in *Christianity for the Tough Minded* (Minneapolis: Bethany Fellowship, Inc., 1973), pp. 21-22. Montgomery states: "Pantheism . . . is neither true nor false; it is something much worse, viz., entirely trivial. We had little doubt that the universe was here anyway; by giving it a new name ("God") we explain nothing. We actually commit the venerable intellectual sin of Word Magic, wherein the naming of something is supposed to give added power either to the thing named or to the semantic magician himself" (*Ibid.,* p. 22).

4. Hildebert of Lavardin, cited in A. W. Tozer, *The Knowledge of the Holy* (New York: Harper & Row, 1961), p. 80.

5. A. W. Tozer, *The Pursuit of God* (Harrisburg: Christian Publications, Inc., 1948), p. 35.

6. John goes on to say that *even those who pierced Him* will see Him at the second advent (Rev. 1:7; see Zech. 12:10; John 19:37). Evidently, the "every eye" that will see Him includes not only those who are on earth at that time but all creatures. The currently popular idea that all people will be able to see Christ when He comes because of *television* is sheer nonsense unless those in Hades have access to cable TV. Besides, a quick look at the destruction caused by the seal, trumpet, and bowl judgments in Revelation makes it clear that by the end of the tribulation when the second coming occurs, few people will still be watching television, even if the stations are transmitting (see Matt. 24:21-22). Christ compared His coming to lightning which comes from the east and flashes to the west (Matt. 24:27; Luke 17:24).

CHAPTER 10

1. Louis Berkof, *Systematic Theology* (Grand Rapids: Wm. B. Eerdmans Publishing Co., 1939), pp. 29-34.

2. John R. W. Stott, *Basic Christianity* (Downers Grove, Illinois: Inter-Varsity Press, 1958), p. 73.

3. Cornelius Van Til, *The New Modernism* (3rd. ed.; Nutley, New Jersey: Presbyterian and Reformed Publishing Company, 1946), pp. 4-7. However, they also denied the idea of a temporal creation, and this logically leads to a God who is not so transcendent after all. Van Til says:

"Accordingly the transcendence doctrine of one who rejects causal creation cannot be that of a God who is really free. It must always be the transcendence of a God who is necessarily related to the universe" (*Ibid.*, pp. 6-7).

4. Rem B. Edwards, *Reason and Religion* (New York: Harcourt Brace Jovanovich, Inc., 1972), p. 211. See also Ewert H. Cousins, ed., *Process Theology* (New York: Newman Press, 1971).

5. As Berkhof (*Systematic Theology*, pp. 29-30) notes, Hegel and Schleiermacher also fit into the immanence extreme since they played down the transcendence of God and denied revelation. They essentially said that all one needs to know about God can be discovered in the depths of one's being.

6. Robert E. Morosco, "Theological Implications of Fear: The Grasshopper Complex," *Journal of Psychology and Theology*, I (April 1973), 44.

7. A. W. Tozer, *The Knowledge of the Holy* (New York: Harper & Row, 1961), p. 77. Morosco ("Theological Implications," p. 50) gives a scriptural list of positive effects which result from the fear of God. Some of these include wisdom, happiness, displeasure with evil, and righteousness.

8. Kenneth Grahame, *The Wind in the Willows* (New York: Charles Scribner's Sons, 1933), p. 127.

CHAPTER 11

1. This list is set forth by Lewis Sperry Chafer in a section called "The Riches of Divine Grace" in his *Systematic Theology* (8 vols.; Dallas: Dallas Seminary Press, 1948), III, 234-65.

2. Another difference relates to sanctification. On the one hand, believers are positionally sanctified, that is, they have been *completely* set apart from the world to God in their position in Christ. But on the other hand, there is an experiential or progressive sense of sanctification. This is a *process* which continues throughout a believer's life, and it is related to his growth in the Lord. The normal Christian life should have an overall trend in which experience comes gradually closer to position.

CHAPTER 12

1. Charles Caldwell Ryrie, *A Survey of Bible Doctrine* (Chicago: Moody Press, 1972), p. 38.

2. Norman L. Geisler and William E. Nix, *A General Introduction to the Bible* (Chicago: Moody Press, 1968), p. 27.

3. We do not know why God has allowed textual variants to creep into the manuscripts. No doubt the original manuscripts would be worshiped had they been preserved. God has chosen to use frail and fallible men in the preservation of His revelation, but at the same time His providence ensured that the text remained free of serious corruption. Because of the quantity and quality of the manuscripts, textual criticism can be applied in the virtual reconstruction of the original text.

4. One of the places where this analogy breaks down is the fact that Christ was never corrupted, but the Bible has been partly corrupted by impurities which came into the text. As we said before, however, we can still reconstruct the text to a point of substantial purity with the aid of textual criticism.

5. A. W. Tozer, *The Divine Conquest* (Harrisburg: Christian Publications, Inc., 1950), p. 79.

Inspirational Victor Books for Your Enjoyment